Unequal Pay for Women and Men

Unequal Pay for Women and Men

Evidence from the British Birth Cohort Studies

Heather Joshi and Pierella Paci

with Gerald Makepeace and Jane Waldfogel

The MIT Press
Cambridge, Massachusetts
London, England

This book was set in Palatino on the Monotype "Prism Plus" PostScript Imagesetter by Asco Trade Typesetting Ltd., Hong Kong.

Printed and bound in the United States of America.

Library of Congress Cataloging-in-Publication Data

Joshi, Heather.
  Unequal pay for women and men : evidence from the British birth cohort studies / Heather Joshi and Pierella Paci, with Gerald Makepeace and Jane Waldfogel.
      p.   cm.
  Includes bibliographical references (p.   ) and index.
  ISBN 0-262-10068-1 (hc : alk. paper)
  1. Wages—Women—Great Britain—Longitudinal studies. 2. Sex discrimination in employment—Great Britain—Longitudinal studies. 3. Income distribution—Great Britain—Longitudinal studies. I. Paci, Pierella, 1957– . II. Title.
HD6061.2.G7J67   1998
331.2'153'0941—dc21   98-23559
                                                                CIP

In memory of
Frank Spooner
1948–1972
Maria Lilia Paci
1961–1994

Contents

Tables

Figures

Abbreviations

BCS70	1970 British Cohort Study
BHPS	British Household Panel Study (started 1991)
D_f	Index of discrimination: percentage by which average woman's pay would change if remunerated at men's levels
D_m	Index of discrimination: change in the average man's pay if remunerated at women's rates (expressed as percentage of average woman's pay)
EC	European Community
ECJ	European Court of Justice
EEO	Equal Employment Opportunity
EOC	Equal Opportunities Commission (U.K.)
ESRC	Economic and Social Research Council
FES	Family Expenditure Survey (recurrent cross section)
GHS	General Household Survey (recurrent cross-section)
ILO	International Labor Organization
MRC	Medical Research Council (also used here as short for MRC National Survey of Health and Development of the 1946 birth cohort)
NCDS	National Child Development Study of the 1958 birth cohort
NES	New Earnings Survey
NICHD	National Institute for Child Health and Development (U.S.)
NLSY	National Longitudinal Survey of Youth (U.S.)
NLSYW	National Longitudinal Survey of Young Women (U.S.)

NSHD   National Survey of Health and Development 1946 birth cohort
        (also known as MRC NSHD or MRC)
PMS   Perinatal Mortality Survey
SSRU   Social Statistics Research Unit, City University, London (home
        of NCDS and BCS70)
WES   Women and Employment Survey, 1980

Preface

It is a coincidence that the two main authors of this book (nearly) share years of birth with the two cohorts studied, 1946 and 1958. Neither of us managed to be born in the exact week of the studies (Heather Joshi was born in 1946 and Pierella Paci in 1957), but we have personal experience of the changes we study. Our entries into motherhood in the 1980s and 1990s respectively have not prevented our carrying out the work described in this book. They have given us first-hand experience of the market for child care and the appreciation of our husbands' sharing of parental responsibilities. We have also been more fortunate than many of our contemporaries studied in this book, in working for employers with equal opportunities policies and family-friendly practices. These include the tolerance of our colleagues of our dual roles. We look forward to our daughters and sons finding the world a more gender-neutral place than the one on which we report here.

The research reported on these pages has had a long gestation and several funders. Our work on the MRC National Survey of Health and Development started in 1979 while Heather Joshi was at the ESRC-funded Centre for Population Studies at the London School of Hygiene and Tropical Medicine. We are grateful to Dr. James Douglas and his successors, Professor John Colley and Professor Michael Wadsworth, for permission to use the 1946 study, and to their staff for their help during the process of coding and extracting data. Máire Ní Bhrolcháin, Colin Newell, and Ian Timæus were all colleagues at the London School of Hygiene and Tropical Medicine involved in creating a database covering women's employment and fertility histories. We also had help at this stage from Kathleen Kiernan and Sandra Eldridge. Marie-Louise Newell joined the team to work on the analysis of pay differentials, for which the Department of Employment provided some funding. These findings were circulated as a research report from the Institute of Employment Research,

University of Warwick (Joshi and Newell 1989). Then and now, the views expressed are our own, and not necessarily those of the Department.

Funding for the research reported here—a re-analysis of pay differentials in the 1946 cohort, and one of the first analyses of pay data collected from the 1958 cohort in 1991, also came from the Employment Department, as it was, by 1994, known. By that time, Heather Joshi was based in SSRU, City University, the home of the NCDS Study. Gerald Makepeace, Peter Dolton, and Jane Waldfogel were consultants on that project, and Pierella Paci was given leave from the economics department of City University to work as the research officer on the study. Again, we had help from colleagues with preparing data: Peter Shepherd, Kate Smith, Clare Ward, and Mahmood Sadigh in particular. We have also had invaluable help from Dina Maher, Catherine Smallwood, Kevin Dodwell, and Jean Pitt-Jones in preparing the manuscript. All these contributions are gratefully acknowledged. Special thanks are due to John Charlton for making available the data for figure 1.1 and to Francine Blau for sharing some of the data needed to produce figure 1.2. Romana Peronaci created figure 3.2, under her funding from the Leverhulme Trust. We have also had extensive and helpful advice from three anonymous referees.

Our co-authors, Gerry Makepeace and Jane Waldfogel, have not only contributed general advice, but have made specific contributions to the present text. Gerry Makepeace, professor of economics, University College Wales, Cardiff, is a co-author of chapter 3, for which he devised the series of econometric tests and performed the estimates reported. Jane Waldfogel, assistant professor at Columbia School of Social Work, New York, is a co-author of chapters 1 and 6. The report of our original research project, delivered in March 1995 to the Employment Department, was published in 1996 by what had become the Department for Education and Employment (Paci and Joshi 1996). Meanwhile, an earlier version of what is now chapter 5 had been published as part of the Equal Opportunities Commission's conference volume on the Economics of Equal Opportunities (Paci et al. 1995). The version presented here (and in the DfEE report) includes an extra variable, industry, coded late and, unfortunately, incompletely, so that it also covers a smaller sample. The present text builds on the DfEE report, and has revised and extended it. Econometric estimates for chapters 4 and 6 are new. Introductory material has now increased to fill the first three chapters, with more material on equal pay policy and the international context in chapter 1, and more about the birth cohort studies in chapter 3. The concluding chapter has also been enlarged to include a discussion of policy implications.

Throughout, we have tried to avoid using the term "work," as if only paid activities counted as such. In another attempt to avoid devaluing time not spent in paid employment, we have also tried to avoid the expressions "part-time women" and "full-time women." These are widely and easily used. Where we have lapsed, it is to avoid stylistic tedium, not to endorse the idea that people with part-time jobs are in any way diminished human beings.

In another, sadder, coincidence, the two main authors of this book share the unusual and deeply mourned experience of having each lost a sibling to accidents on the road. We dedicate this book to their memory.

1

What Do We Know about Unequal Pay?*

Why Does Gender Pay Inequality Matter?

Time is precious, for both men and women, but is it as valuable for women as men? For most of recorded history, men's pay has tended to be higher than women's. This both reflects and underpins their different roles, men's authority tending to be superior socially as well as economically. Egalitarian values of the late twentieth century seek to ensure equal opportunity to economic participation, regardless of gender (or race). What may once have been an economic rationale for employers to prefer men has been outdated by the knowledge-based technology of the post-industrial economy. This puts more of a premium on the power of workers' brains than of their muscles. Just as unequal pay underpins economic and social inequality, its elimination is the key to their removal. No amount of training, maternity leave, or child-care provisions, for example, will change women's economic status if treatment in pay remains unequal—if the market values men's time more than women's. Are the policies designed to establish equal pay succeeding? Can they succeed? Should we always expect women's wages to lag behind? Is unequal pay just a fact of life?

In a market economy, the rate of pay per hour puts a price on people's time. If the market in human time is operating neutrally and efficiently, it will pay the same rate to persons of equal skill and productivity in equally desirable jobs. This is generally considered fair. Wages will differ among people as do the skills they offer. But they can also vary for a host of other reasons. Higher pay for men than women is just one of many ways in which wage rates have often been observed to differ. This gap in the price of time for men compared to women determines not only who waits for whom, but has enormous consequences for their respective incomes,

---

* Jane Waldfogel is a co-author of his chapter.

Table 1.1
Men per 100 women in the labor force, selected industrial countries in the postwar period

	1950	1982	1994
Anglo-Saxon countries			
United Kingdom	226	156	129
United States	246	134	118
Canada	369	144	123
Australia	346	170	136
New Zealand	325	189[a]	127
Continental Europe			
Austria	160	158	138[b]
France	179	159	123
Germany (W.)	185	162	141
Greece	211	212[c]	168[b]
Italy	294	196	171
Netherlands	327	228	143
Switzerland	236	183	131[d]
Scandinavian countries			
Denmark	198	125[c]	117
Finland	146	112	113
Iceland	251	189	114
Norway	269	137	120
Sweden	280	129	108

Sources: OECD 1985, table 1.2; *ILO Yearbook of Labour Statistics*, 1995, table 1; ONS 1997.
Notes: a. 1981; b. 1993; c. 1980; d. 1990.

for which parent takes time off work to look after children, for the domestic division of labor, for the incentive to women to get educated, for their financial dependence on the family, and for their vulnerability to the risk of poverty.

Paid work never was the exclusive province of men, but the proportion of the workforce who are women has been increasing in all industrialized countries, as illustrated in table 1.1.

In 1950, there were at least two men for every woman in the labor force of almost all the countries shown in table 1.1. The exceptions still had a large agricultural sector. By 1982 the ratio was down to one and a half man per woman in most places, including the United Kingdom. By the 1990s there were still more men than women in all these labor forces, but the margin was narrowing. In Scandinavia the ratio approached 1.1 man per woman, similar to levels already established in the socialist economies (not shown). This changing composition of the labor force reflects both declining participation rates by men and rising participation by women. More detail of the latter, for British women, appears in chapter 3 (figure 3.2). Another way to give more detail about British trends is presented in figure 1.1, which shows how the numbers in employment were composed, not only of men and women but of the self-employed, full-time employees, and part-time employees.[1] The main point to note is that the increase in women's employment between 1961 and 1991 consisted largely of part-time jobs. By 1991 there were almost as many part-time jobs as full-time for British women. This aspect of the trend is far from universal, but it means that the study of British women's employment needs to recognize this important division in the labor force.

It can also be argued that the differential wages of men and women are a consequence of the different ways they typically allocate their time over the life cycle. Women take the brunt of the domestic burden because they face low wages. Women face low wages because many of them choose not to commit themselves wholeheartedly to the labor force.[2] These mechanisms may work in both directions.[3]

On the view that the primary source of the differential behavior is unequal treatment in the labor market, some women are trapped in domesticity. The signal from the market is distorted, and they are discouraged from developing their productive potential or using what they have to the full (or their menfolk can argue that it is not worth it). In this case, unequal pay is not only unfair but inefficient; policies ensuring that men and women face equal opportunities and equal pay should overcome outdated prejudices. On the other view, the different but complementary life courses of men and women are an efficient way of organizing human affairs, which would arise even if the labor market treated equivalently qualified persons identically.[4] In this view, unequal pay between men and women would persist, reflecting differential acquisition of human capital, and need not reflect discriminatory treatment. There would be a limit to the changes, if any, that equal pay legislation could bring about.

Differences in the rate of pay received by men and women are thus important from the points of view of the functioning of the economy and of fairness—efficiency as well as equity. Equity within the labor market would entail that equally productive workers (assuming equally desirable jobs) receive equal pay, irrespective of gender, age, or race. The efficient allocation of resources requires that workers receive a wage equal to their value product, at the margin. For the labor market to operate efficiently, equally productive workers (with the same preferences) should receive

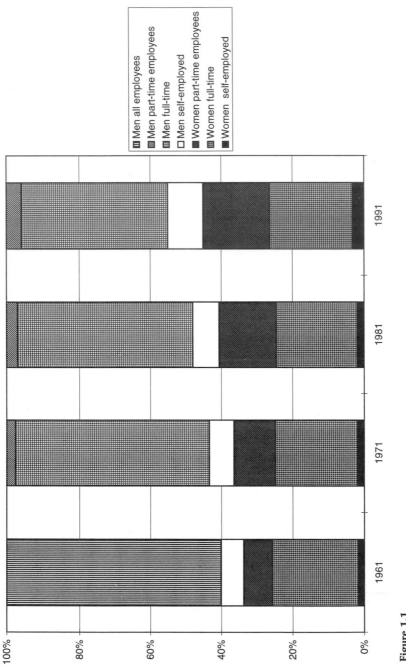

Figure 1.1
Composition of the British workforce, 1961–91

equal pay. If they do not, it will, among other things, reinforce differences in the time each group allocates to paid and unpaid work, to acquiring skills and building up human capital. Low returns on the latter for women may well inhibit the development of their full potential to contribute to the economy. The ensuing reliance on her partner's earnings leads to economic vulnerability within, and especially after, marriage (Cigno 1991; Joshi, Davies, and Land 1996).

However, neither allocative efficiency nor horizontal equity requires that all women and all men should be paid identically, even on average. Equal pay legislation is not necessarily ineffective if there is a gap between men's and women's pay. It may just be that women and men are not identical in terms of the productive endowment they bring to the marketplace. Alternatively, they may attach different importance to nonpecuniary aspects of the job (as asserted, for some women, by Hakim [1991, 1996] and suggested by Killingsworth [1987, 1990] and Sloane and Theodossiou [1994]). Killingsworth suggests that different rates of pay for men and women could arise in a nondiscriminatory market because of taste differences. If the differences in preferences were conditioned by social discrimination, however, giving women different role models and expectations to those of men, they might still not be fair or efficient.

Length of employment experience is one crucial factor that might be expected to raise men's productivity over women's, because of learning-by-doing as well as formal on-the-job training. Women tend to interrupt their employment records for domestic reasons, whereas most men do not. An account of the male-female pay gap therefore needs evidence on employment experience linked to earnings. This is not available in the standard British cross-sectional national surveys, such as the New Earnings Survey, the Family Expenditure Survey, or the General Household Survey. The British birth cohort studies are among the few large-scale data sets that permit the employment record of a worker to be brought into the analysis of earnings. They also contain a great deal of other material that can enrich the investigation. Our evidence is taken from two prospective birth cohort studies, the Medical Research Council's National Survey of Health and Development (MRC) and the National Child Development Study (NCDS). As described in more detail in chapter 3, these studies have collected a wealth of information throughout the subjects' lives from their birth in 1946 and 1958 respectively. We take this important longitudinal evidence up to the 1970s and the 1990s, when the cohort members are in their early thirties. Their wages are observed at points spanning a period between the early days of equal pay legislation and what may be its maturity.

This book focuses on the unique testimony these two cohort studies bring to the issue of differential pay between British men and women. They enable us to investigate the individual histories that lie behind their unequal rates of pay, and whether the inequality begins in the home or labor market. We ask how far the narrowing of the pay gap over a period when equal treatment legislation was being consolidated could be accounted for by a reduction of unequal treatment of men and women. It could also reflect a catching up by women born in the postwar years with men's qualifications and earning power. We also investigate differential treatment in different types of jobs. Women's pay in part-time jobs is particularly unfavorable. We investigate how this relates to their family responsibilities.

Before turning to the empirical analysis in the bulk of the book, we look first at definitions of discrimination and then at the gender gap in wages in a broader empirical and theoretical context.

Discrimination in the Courtroom and in Economics

The notion of discrimination is not defined in law in the same way as in economic analysis. The British Equal Pay Act of 1970, for example, made it illegal to offer different wages for the same work on the grounds of sex. This resulted in the disappearance of different nationally negotiated rates for men and women, but pay differentials remained, particularly between types of job done mainly by women and less segregated types of employment. This type of gap was addressed in the legislation of several countries by laws enjoining equal pay for work of equal value. In the United Kingdom there was the Equal Pay for Equal Value Amendment of the Equal Pay Act of 1983. Under the amended law, a woman can claim that her low pay is discriminatory by pointing to a male comparator doing comparable work for greater pay. The Employment Tribunal accepts, as evidence of discrimination, case by case detail on what work is actually performed and, since the Equal Value Amendment, assesses whether the skills are comparable, often in formal job evaluations.

The economist, by contrast, does secondary analysis of less specific material for a large number of observations, not necessarily people employed by the same firm. Unequal treatment is deemed to occur if, with equivalent productivity, workers are not in fact equally rewarded. The attributes of relevance are not specific to particular jobs. Rather they are more general determinants of earning power, which ought to bring an equivalent return throughout a competitive labor market. Wage differentials adjusted for characteristics such as education and experience are conventionally used in the economics literature to measure discrimination. This methodology, originated by Oaxaca (1973) and Blinder (1973), is explained in detail in chapter 2. Econometric analyses have been used in U.S. courtrooms, where pleas can be made in class action suits on behalf of groups of claimants, but regressions have not as yet been admitted as evidence in any British tribunal (Bloom and Killingsworth 1982; Killingsworth 1993).

The Legislative Framework of Equal Pay

The practice of paying men and women at different rates has a very long history. For economic as well as ideological reasons this tradition has become increasingly anachronistic in the twentieth century. The political principle of equal treatment in law and citizenship suggested that male and female workers should be treated equally. There were also broad forces of economic change increasing the demand for women's labor, without which merely legislating for equal pay was unlikely to have wrought much success. The technological change toward the postindustrial economy created a demand for women's as well as men's brainpower. Significant features of this technology transformation include the contraceptive as well as the computer (Bellace 1991). Mincer (1985) and OECD (1988) summarize international evidence on the increase of women's labor-force participation alongside their relative wages. As Mincer points out, these can also be related to changes in fertility and family structure.[5]

As early as 1919, the principle of equal pay for work of equal value by men and women was recognized in the preamble to the charter of the International Labor Organization. It was reaffirmed in ILO Convention 100 of 1951. Article 119 of the Treaty of Rome, which initiated the European Community in 1957, required member states to maintain the principle of equal pay for equal work; this was designed to ensure a level playing field between countries with and without such laws (McCrudden 1991). Individual countries started to implement the principle(s) by bringing in various types of legislation (surveyed in table 1.2). These were equal pay laws, backed by equal opportunity measures that aimed to remove discriminatory hiring and promotion practice.

Soon it was realized that for women with responsibilities for children, these measures may not be sufficient to remove barriers to equal pay, if

Table 1.2
Equal pay and equal employment opportunity (EEO) policies in Scandinavian, continental European, and Anglo-Saxon countries

	Year	Policy
Scandinavian countries		
Denmark	1976	Equal pay act
	1986	Equal pay / EEO legislation
Norway	1978	Equal pay / EEO legislation
	1978	Equal pay / EEO collective bargaining agreement
Sweden	1960	Collective Agreement on Equal Pay
	1980	Equal pay / EEO legislation
	1983	Equal pay / EEO collective bargaining agreement
Continental European countries		
Austria	1979	Equal pay act
	1985	EEO legislation
Belgium	1975	Equal Pay
	1985, 1987, 1990	EEO amendments and decrees
France	1972	Equal pay
	1983	Equal opportunity legislation
Germany	1980	Equal pay act
	1994	EEO legislation
Italy	1960	Equal pay collective bargaining agreement
	1964	Equal pay legislation
	1977	EEO legislation
	1983	Government order re: EEO
	1991	EEO legislation
Anglo-Saxon countries		
Australia	1969	Equal pay ruling by gov. commission
	1972	Equal pay ruling by gov. commission
	1984, 1986, 1987	EEO legislation
Britain	1970	Equal pay act (passed)
	1975	Equal pay act (in effect)
	1975	EEO legislation
	1983	Equal pay act (amended)
	1986	EEO legislation (amended)
Canada	1951	Equal pay provinces (starts in Ontario)
	1971	Federal EEO office established
	1977	EEO; comparable worth (starts in Quebec)
	1986	EEO legislation
	1985–	Pay equity legislation (provinces)
United States	1963	Equal pay act
	1964	EEO legislation (civil rights Title VII)
	1968	EEO executive order
	1972	EEO legislation

Sources: Blau and Kahn 1994; EC Employment Observatory 1994; Gunderson and Robb 1991; OECD 1988.

there are also barriers to labor-force participation. Legislation mandating or facilitating some "family-friendly" provisions, which made it easier to combine employment and child rearing, was then implemented. This is listed in table 1.3.

Equal Pay and Family-Friendly Policy in Great Britain

In Great Britain, equal treatment of men and women in the labor market has been enshrined in law since the mid-1970s, having been under discussion since a Trade Union Congress motion in 1888. Arguments against its introduction included the notion that men—but not women—needed to be paid a "family wage" because of their responsibilities for supporting dependants.[6] Another was that employers would not be able to afford raising women's pay. As recently as 1946, a Royal Commission had rejected the idea of equal pay for men and women, but it was finally introduced for the civil service in 1961.

In 1970 Barbarn Castle, Secretary of State for Employment in a Labour government, secured support for the principle of equal treatment. The resulting Equal Pay Act, passed in 1970, came into full force in 1975, at the same time as the enactment of two pieces of legislation intended to back it up: the Sex Discrimination Act and the Employment Protection Act. The first prohibited discrimination in hiring, and the second established, among other things, the right to a job-protected maternity leave for certain workers.[7] The Equal Opportunities Commission (EOC) was set up under the Sex Discrimination Act to monitor the implementation of the laws, help complainants bring cases, and advise the Government

Once enacted, equal opportunity policy received little active encouragement from the government led by Margaret Thatcher. She came to power in 1979 and embarked upon a different labor-market agenda— deregulation. This involved the decentralization or dismantling of collective bargaining (Hunter and Rimmer 1995; Disney et al. 1995; Brown 1993). It also involved the eventual abolition of what minimum wage machinery there was in the form of wages councils. In the United States, government contracts were used to induce suppliers to adopt equal opportunity practices. In Britain, central and local government found themselves increasingly subcontracting work to agencies and contractors, under compulsory competitive tendering (CCT). The immediate objective was to cut costs rather than improve human resource management. The general aim was to achieve a flexible labor market more like that already existing in the United States.

Table 1.3
Maternity leave, parental leave, and child-care provisions in 1994 in Scandinavian, continental European, and Anglo-Saxon countries

| | Leave provisions | | Child-care provisions | | |
| | | | % in formal care | | Cost of care as % female earnings[d] |
	Maternity weeks	Paternity weeks	<3 years	3–school age	
Scandinavia					
Denmark	18	10–52	60	79	8
Finland	17.5	26–156	25	50	7
Norway	a	52	—	46	13
Sweden	a	62	32	63	7
Continental Europe					
Austria	16	112	3	69	11
Belgium	15	130	18–19	95+	0
Germany	14	156	4	68[c]	3
France	16	0–156	33	99	0
Italy	22	26	6	95	7
Anglo-Saxon countries					
Australia	52	52	—	43	6
Britain	14–40	(none)	7	66	28
Canada	17	10	10	33	(na)
New Zealand	a	52	—	42	20
United States	b	12	26	71	22

Sources: EC Employment Observatory 1994; Bradshaw et al. 1996; Waldfogel 1997; Heitlinger 1993.
Notes
a. These countries have no separate maternity leave provisions; maternity leave falls under parental leave.
b. The United States has no separate maternity or paternity leave provisions; these fall under family leave. Note also that leave in the United States is unpaid, in contrast to the other countries shown here.
c. Percentages are for the former West Germany; provision in the former East Germany was higher.
d. Calculated by Bradshaw et al. 1996, this measure is the average child-care cost for one child age 2 years, 11 months, divided by the average earnings for a lone mother.

Nevertheless the Equal Pay Act was amended in 1983 to strengthen the requirement of equal pay for work of comparable value. This change was forced upon the British government in compliance with the European Community (EC) Directive on Equal Pay of 1975, which extended Article 119 to equal pay for work of equal value. For similar reasons, the maternity leave legislation was amended several times, most recently in 1994. To comply with a decision in the European Court of Justice (ECJ), maternity leave rights were extended to all workers regardless of tenure in the job or part-time status.

European Community law has also led to the gradual extension of employment rights to Britain's relatively numerous and mainly female part-time workers. Practices that put part-timers at a disadvantage are viewed as "indirect discrimination" (Hanlon 1996; Hakim 1996). Two ECJ judgments in 1993 paved the way for part-timers to claim the right to join their employer's pension scheme (if they can afford it). In 1995, regulations were brought in to extend protection against unfair dismissal to workers employed less than sixteen hours per week. These rights still only apply to workers with more than two years' service. At the time of writing, the two-year qualification is itself being challenged in the courts as indirectly discriminatory.[8]

The draft European directive to strengthen the rights of part-time and fixed-term workers (1994) would have consolidated the rights of these vulnerable workers. It was not the first piece of European social legislation to be vetoed by the British government that came to power in 1979. Indeed given Mrs. Thatcher's campaign of labor-market deregulation, it is especially pertinent to see how equal pay fared in an open climate if not a level playing field.

The Equal Pay Act (1970) simply makes it illegal for an employer to pay different rates to men and women performing the same (or, since 1983, comparable) work. Thus an important limitation of any such legislation is that it does not address inequities of pay between those working for different employers. A second limitation of Britain's Equal Pay Act is that the enforcement process is fairly cumbersome (McCrudden 1991; Heitlinger 1993). An aggrieved individual must file a complaint to initiate the process, which can often take more than five years to resolve.

Cases under the Equal Pay and Sex Discrimination Acts are heard by industrial tribunals consisting of representatives of employers and unions, who receive little specific training on sex discrimination. Expert evidence often takes many months to assemble and assess. In contrast to the United States and Canada, there are no class-action suits, which automatically transfer any ruling obtained by particular complainants to others in similar situations. There is no legal aid for individuals claiming sex discrimination. In practice, cases are seldom taken up without the support of a union or the Equal Opportunities Commission, but these have sufficient resources to bring only a limited number of cases.

This political climate may explain why Britain's provisions for family-friendly policies are limited as well. Until recently (1994), the maternity leave provisions covered fewer than half of all working women, and there are no statutory provisions for paternity leave or parental leave (i.e., leave that may be taken by either parent to care for, or arrange for the care of, a child). Britain also has very little provision of government support for child care. This results in a shortage of places, especially for children under 3. In the early 1990s, only 7% of British children under the age of 3 were enrolled in formal child care. This contrasts with figures for countries such as France (33%), Sweden (32%), and the United States (26%). Because public provision is limited, British women are more likely than those in other countries to have to purchase child care privately, leading to higher costs of care. Nor does the government provide any tax relief for these costs.

Institutions in Other Industrial Countries

To place the British experience in context, it is useful to consider how some other countries have addressed unequal pay of men and women and how successful their efforts to reconcile the inequities have been. We consider three groups of countries: the Scandinavian countries; the continental European countries; and the Anglo-Saxon countries including Britain, Canada, Australia, and the United States. Tables 1.2 and 1.3 summarize the institutional framework in these three groups.

The Scandinavian countries, as a group, have the strongest legislative framework and display the closest overall gender pay ratios. In addition to collective bargaining agreements that tend to precede equal pay legislation, these countries typically have very extensive policy supports in the areas of maternity leave, parental leave, and child care. Taking the example of Sweden, its institutional framework includes: labor and management initiatives as early as 1960 to phase in the elimination of negotiated pay disparities between men and women; an equal pay law passed in 1980, instituting an equal pay ombudsman; some extremely generous maternity leave and parental leave provisions, including the right for either parent to return to work part-time if desired; and very extensive public sector child care.

As a result of these provisions, Scandinavian women are more likely to be attached to an employer post-childbirth and are less likely to have the breaks in employment so typical of British women (Joshi 1996). Another important difference is that Scandinavian laws and union contracts effectively mandate equal pay for part-time work, permitting full-time jobs to be done at the same rate on reduced hours. As a result, there is no part-time wage penalty.[9]

Another factor important to understanding the Scandinavian case is the concentration of women in public sector jobs. This makes it easier for government policy to fix their pay relative to men's. It also leads to the general compression of the wage distribution within which there is not much scope for gender differences (see Rosholm and Smith 1996 on Denmark).

The continental European countries also have equal pay legislation and (mainly) a stronger framework of support for maternity leave, parental leave, and child care than is the case in Britain. In France and Italy, for example, provisions include: equal pay legislation; generous parental leave, particularly in Italy; and universal child care from the age of 3. But there are important differences among these countries as well. In France, child care is widely available for children under 3, while in Italy the proportion of children under 3 in formal child care is very low at 6% (Bradshaw et al. 1996). In Germany, the supply of child care is extremely limited, nor is it easy for women of school-age children to work full-time given the school schedule and retail business hours (Ostner 1993).

Equal pay policies also range widely in the Anglo-Saxon countries. The United States was one of the earliest to pass equal pay legislation, in 1963, but with relatively little effect, given the decentralized nature of wage setting. As in Britain, the enforcement mechanism is fairly cumbersome, and the applicability of the law is limited in that it addresses inequity of pay only within, not across, firms. Australia, on the other hand, has a national comparable worth policy (1972), in addition to its 1969 equal pay legislation. This took dramatic effect, due to its centralized pay-setting system which, until recent deregulation, covered 90% or more of all employees (Blau and Kahn 1994; see also Hunter and Rimmer 1995). The United States and Canada have pursued comparable worth policies as well, but not on a national basis. In the United States, comparable worth has been advanced in several states, most notably Washington and Minnesota. In Canada, the first province to adopt comparable worth was

Ontario, in 1987 (Willborn 1989 and 1991; Killingsworth 1990; and Heitlinger 1993).

The Anglo-Saxon countries also vary in the provisions for maternity leave, parental leave, and child care. The United States was the latest to introduce maternity leave and parental leave: the Family and Medical Leave Act was not signed into law until 1993. All the Anglo-Saxon countries rely on private child care to a larger extent than the Scandinavian or continental European countries. The United States places the greatest emphasis on private as opposed to public provision. This is supported to some extent by tax credits or deductions for child-care expenses; there are also subsidies for low-income families. Australia, on the other hand, funds more care directly, and as a result costs for parents are much lower than they are in the United States or Britain (Bradshaw et al. 1996).

International Evidence on Women's Relative Wages

These differences in policy environments are reflected in the relative excess of men's pay over women's, as depicted in figure 1.2. Throughout this book we express pay differentials as percentages of the lower-paid group in the comparison. This practice, commonly used in the econometric analysis of pay differentials, describes a situation where men's pay averaged $5 to women's $3, as a 67% differential. The $2 gap is expressed as a fraction of the women's $3. The situation can be equivalently expressed relative to men's pay, as a 40% gap, $2 as a fraction of $5, and women's relative pay as 60%. This way of expressing the ratio may be more familiar, but given the indices of discrimination defined in chapter 2, it is a less helpful starting point for the analyses that follow.[10] In this book, men's wages are systematically compared to women's.

Because of the varying definitions and coverage of these series (see note to figure 1.2), their relative levels cannot be taken as seriously as the speed of the transition toward more equal rates of pay that they all display. Virtually all industrial countries (except Japan, not shown) have seen some reduction in the men's lead over women's pay since the 1960s. For some the reduction was gradual (e.g., Sweden and the United States). For others the reduction was concentrated in a few years around the time of an equal pay initiative (e.g., the United Kingdom, Australia). The spurt in Denmark, which precedes the Danish Equal Pay Act, reflects an equal pay initiative taken by the employers and unions.

In the United Kingdom, the series for full-timers in manual occupations shows a rapid decrease from around 1.58 in 1970 to 1.35 shortly after the introduction of the Equal Pay Act in 1977. The ratio rebounded to around 1.38 in 1978 and stagnated until the late 1980s, when it again started to decline, gradually reaching 1.28 in 1991 and 1.25 in 1994.

Women's pay relative to men's has risen most sharply in the countries with stronger equal pay legislation and enforcement, centralized wage setting, and stronger maternity leave, parental leave, part-time protections, and child-care policies. This group includes Scandinavia and parts of the continent, such as France and Belgium, as well as the two Antipodean Anglo-Saxon countries, Australia and New Zealand.

Gender pay gaps have fallen the least in the countries that lack one or more elements of the above set of policies. This group includes Britain (lacking effective enforcement, parental leave, and child care); the United States (until recently lacking parental leave and child care); Germany (lacking child care); and Switzerland (lacking equal pay legislation until 1981, and even this has had limited effects).

The policies considered reflect part of the range of ways the costs of social reproduction are distributed. As reviewed by Folbre (1994), they are shared between the state and the family, and, within the family, between men and women. The least egalitarian arrangements appear to be in Japan, which ranks near the bottom of the list of industrial countries in men's share of domestic work as well as women's relative pay (Juster and Stafford 1991).

The most egalitarian arrangements appear in Scandinavia, where there has been the greatest attempt to "socialize the costs of familyhood" (Esping-Anderson 1990), or "to adopt pro-family policies that were more pro-woman and with fewer restrictions on reproductive choice" (Folbre 1994). As Heitlinger (1993) also points out, it is possible for policies to promote both the family and women's economic equality. Egalitarian pay and egalitarian parenthood lie in the same direction.

The Evolution of Pay Gaps in Britain

In spite of its shortcomings, the British Equal Pay Act coincided with a dramatic narrowing of the pay gap between men and women in Britain. Women's wages in full-time work relative to men's rose sharply in the 1970s, in large part in response to the legislation (Zabalza and Tzannatos 1986; Ermisch et al. 1991; Manning 1996; Harkness and Machin 1995; Harkness 1996; Blackaby et al. 1997; Elias and Gregory 1994). This impact was felt immediately after the Act came into full force, which was after a five-year warning period. It outlawed collective agreements

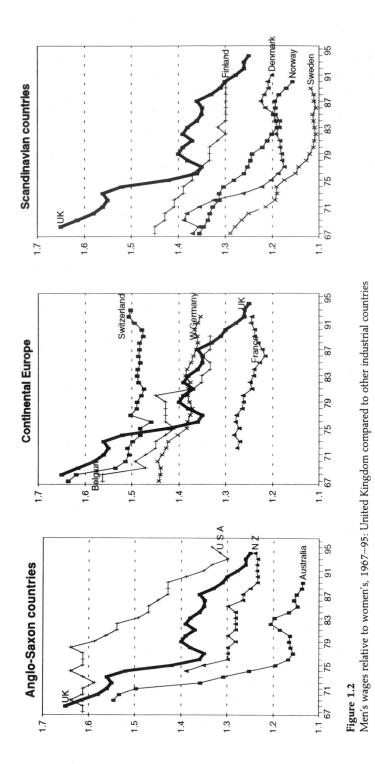

Figure 1.2
Men's wages relative to women's, 1967–95: United Kingdom compared to other industrial countries

The series plotted mainly refer to average hourly earnings in nonagricultural activities, but exact definitions vary.

United Kingdom	full-time manual employees on adult rates—all industries (including overtime)
Finland	manufacturing
Norway	manufacturing
Denmark	mainly manufacturing and construction
Belgium	wages (not salaries) in manufacturing and construction
France	mainly manufacturing and private nondomestic services
Switzerland	includes horticulture; includes family allowances paid by employer
West Germany	excludes services; includes family allowances paid by employer; pre-Germany reunification territory
Australia	full-time, adult, nonmanagerial employees
New Zealand	full-time employees, includes forestry and fisheries
United States	usual weekly earnings of full-timers, all industries

Sources:

United Kingdom	Employment Department: Historical Abstract, Yearbooks of Labour Statistics and subsequent Gazettes
United States	U.S. Bureau of Labor Statistics
Other	ILO Yearbook of Labour Statistics, various years, updated from countries: material supplied by Professor Francine Blau (Blau and Kahn 1994)

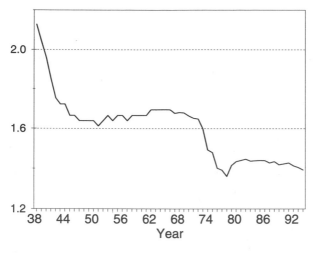

Figure 1.3
Men's hourly wages relative to women's (full-time manual workers, United Kingdom)

stating different rate for males and females, which applied to the large proportion of (full-time) employees at that time, as in Australia, covered by centrally negotiated collective agreements (Willborn 1991).

Recent experience in Britain can be set in a longer historical perspective. Men's pay in manual jobs is thought to have been at least double women's in the prewar part of the century (Joshi et al. 1985). The gender wage gap, as shown in figure 1.3, stayed in the region of two-thirds women's pay between World War II and the Equal Pay Act. This refers to full-time workers in manual occupations. After the act, the gap among this group of workers was a bit bigger than for all occupations in 1978 (41% rather than 38%). It showed no improvement for the following thirteen years at least (see Ermisch et al. 1991).

The New Earnings Survey (NES) is the most reliable source on the differential between the wages of workers of each sex in the full-time labor force as a whole. It is often quoted as indicating levels and trends in their wages. Figure 1.4 reports median hourly earnings for employees in all occupations. The median wage is that which exactly divides the distribution in two. Half are paid more, half less than this amount.[11] Before the Equal Pay Act, the excess of men's full-time pay over women's was 58%. After a small rebound it stood at 40% in 1980 and had fallen to 25% in 1992. The excess of men's full-time wages over women's fell abruptly at the time the Equal Pay Act was enacted in the mid-1970s, and has been falling only gradually since 1980.

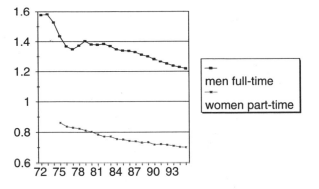

Figure 1.4
Men's hourly pay relative to full-time women's (United Kingdom: NES, median, all occupations)

As shown in figure 1.4, the narrowing in relative full-time wages does not appear to apply to the low rates received by women in part-time jobs. The consistent (though not comprehensive) coverage of these goes back only to 1975, but if anything, they have fallen since then.

Alternative estimates can be drawn from household surveys, averaging all women's pay across full-timers and part-timers. Estimates from the Family Expenditure Survey (FES) put men's relative wages at around 1.67 at the end of the 1960s, when there were relatively few part-timers, and there was not much of a pay penalty.[12] By 1977 the rate stood at 1.43, after which the gap opened again to 1.49 in both 1986 and 1990 (Davies and Joshi 1998).

Figure 1.5 explores the distribution of full-timer's wages a little further. The 1980s were a period when the dispersion within each sex's distribution was widening. We can see whether the wages of men and women in the tails of the distributions were becoming closer or more separated, around the gradually closing gap at the median.

Before the Equal Pay Act, men at the bottom decile of men's full-time hourly earnings were slightly further ahead of the low-paid women at an equivalent point in the women's distribution. The opposite held for high earners, with a relatively smaller gender gap at the top deciles of male and female full-time hourly earnings.

After 1978, this pattern reversed. Low-paid women (at the bottom decile) approached low-paid men's wages faster than at the median, but the gender gap among high full-time earners eroded less fast. By 1992 the excess of men's wages over women's was 20% at the lowest decile and

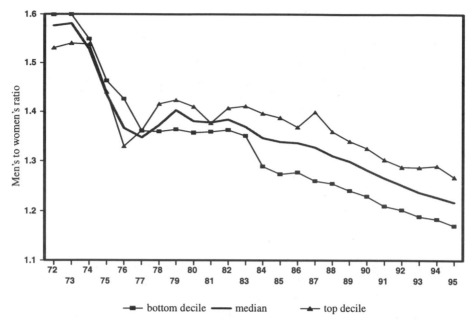

Figure 1.5
Full-time wage differentials, 1972–95 (NES, all occupations)

29% at the highest. At all points of the wage distribution the secular trends in gender ratios are in the same direction, but the change is greatest among the lowest paid. As the dispersion of male wages widened, low-paid men lost ground more than low-paid women full-timers, while among top earners, men outstripped women.

The widening dispersion of wages and earnings over the 1980s is likely to be a result of the government's deregulation policy. For further analyses of these trends, see for example Gosling et al. (1994), Gregg and Machin (1995), Schmitt (1995) and Harkness (1996). For analysis of the ensuing impact on the distribution of income, see Goodman and Webb (1994), Hills (1995), Harkness et al. (1997), and Davies and Joshi (1998).

Between the beginning and the mid-1970s, men's relative pay lead in full-time jobs fell by around 13 percentage points. From the end of the 1970s to the beginning of the 1990s it continued to fall, but more slowly, losing around another eight points. Over the same period, female full-timers' rates rose relative to part-timers', such that the gap between men and women employed part-time actually widened slightly. Was this because discrimination against one group of women declined while it increased for others? Are there other explanations for this trend? This is what we will try to answer.

Plan of the Book

The next chapter explores economic theories about unequal pay. It sets out the conventional econometric approach to the analysis of unequal pay and reviews some of the existing literature in which this approach has been applied to the study of pay differentials in Britain. It sets out the general method adopted in the analyses of the following chapters, and relates the tools of analysis to the various mechanisms that may generate unequal pay. The third chapter introduces the British Birth Cohort Studies and the data sets we have extracted from them to monitor the development of men's and women's pay. It also provides more background material on the changing experience of paid work as well as pay by successive generations of British women. Chapter 4 compares unequal returns to human capital as experienced by men and women from two of the cohorts in their early thirties, asking whether unequal treatment remains unchanged. Chapter 5 brings in job characteristics in addition to personal attributes in as sources of pay differentials among the 1958 cohort. Chapter 6 again compares the two cohorts, on the topic of the relative pay of women with and without children. The circumstances under which motherhood intensifies the pay penalties of gender, and those where it does not, are uncovered. Chapter 7 summarizes our conclusions and their implications for policy toward gender inequality. These are, as we have shown in this chapter, under way, but, as shown in chapters 4 to 6, incomplete.

Unpacking Unequal Pay: Method and Previous Results

In chapter 1, we explained that the existence of a pay gap between men and women may, but does not necessarily, imply discrimination. We introduced the different definitions of discrimination used in law and economics. This chapter expands on the economic concept. It begins by reviewing the theory of discrimination in mainstream economics. It outlines the difficulties encountered in measuring discrimination and the econometric techniques used to address them. We review the empirical results for Britain to date, and then move on to describe the structure of our own analysis.

Discrimination: Types and Causes

According to mainstream economists, there is discrimination in a labor market whenever workers with identical productive characteristics receive different rates of pay because of the population group to which they belong. This is sometimes called "post-entry" discrimination as it occurs after entering the labor market and neglects "pre-entry" discrimination. The latter involves differential access, before labor-market entry, to productivity-enhancing assets, such as education and general training.

Post-entry discrimination entails wage, employment, occupation, or job discrimination. Wage discrimination means that one population group, in our case women, are paid systematically less than people in the rest of the population (men) with equal productivity-related characteristics. In other words, there is discrimination if gender pay differentials are systematically greater than gender differences in productive endowments. Employment discrimination arises when the probability of employment—for any given level of productivity-related characteristics—varies across groups. Job or occupational discrimination occurs if women are restricted from entering certain occupations and are crowded into others for reasons other than their personal preferences. The emphasis of this book is on wage discrimination, but some reference to other forms of discrimination is also made. Wage discrimination may arise for a variety of reasons.[1]

Taste-Based Theories of Discrimination

Becker (1957) proposed a "taste-based" theory of discrimination. In this framework, men may receive preferential treatment because either: (1) employers have a preference for male workers rather than women; (2) male workers "dislike" working alongside women, especially further down the hierarchy; or (3) consumers prefer to deal with men rather than women. The hypothesis of employer discrimination implies that employers do not just maximize profits, but rather, a more general form of utility. This utility increases with profit but decreases with the proportion of women employed. He (or she) then employs women only if the attendant disutility can be compensated by increased profit. This is only possible if the women are paid less. Depending on the prevailing labor-market conditions, such a wage differential may involve the women being paid at or below their marginal value product. In the former case, the men receive more. In the latter, the men receive their marginal value product and the women are, technically, "exploited."[2] Two points are worth noting about employer discrimination. First, it is inefficient, because it results in a misallocation of resources. Second, it cannot survive in the long run, unless the employer enjoys some degree of monopoly power in the output market or all producers in the market have identical taste for discrimination. Otherwise, less discriminatory employers would force the others out by employing a higher percentage of women and therefore reducing labor costs.

With employee and consumer discrimination, the reasons for the existence of a gender gap are different. In the former, employment of women would cause the marginal value product of other employees to decline. In the latter, the marginal value product of women is reduced by the consumer's preference for men. In both cases, the result is employment discrimination, with women being segregated away from discriminatory male employees and/or into those occupations where the consumers are more willing to accept them (e.g., sales and caring occupations). If the employment opportunities for women are relatively limited in number, their "crowding" in these occupations results in a downward pressure on women's wages.

The Effect of Labor-Market Structure

If women are segregated into a relatively small number of occupations and/or firms, abundant supply of labor in these jobs would push down wages and the employer would acquire some degree of monopsony power. This leads to two further interpretations of discrimination.

The "crowding hypothesis," put forward by Edgeworth in 1922 and later developed by Zellner (1972), Bergmann (1971), and others, can be represented in a simple supply and demand framework similar to a normal competitive model. The lower wage of women results from their more abundant supply in some occupations, assuming the workers are equally productive, so the labor demand curve is the same. The underlying idea is that men and women are "noncompeting" groups of workers. This could be due to discrimination or other barriers—including the male-dominated unions—preventing women from joining the uncrowded "male" sectors. In this context, gender is seen as the criterion used for sorting workers into (two) groups and then allocating them into the crowded and un-crowded sector. This theory is therefore consistent with the idea of labor-market segmentation and duality (Chiswick 1973; Stiglitz 1973).

Alternatively, the sorting of men and women into two sectors may reflect supply-side conditions such as systematic gender differences in preferences (Killingsworth 1990) and in the elasticity of labor supply (Manning 1996). The hypothesis behind the first theory is that women have particularly strong preferences for the types of jobs offered in the crowded sector. This means they are prepared to forgo the potentially higher pay offered in the other sectors. Given the element of choice involved in this theory, we refer to it as "voluntary" crowding.

The basis of the second hypothesis is that, due to different family com-mitments, a smaller range of alternative offers, and shorter feasible travel-to-work distances, women tend to be less mobile than men. Thus in employing women employers face an upward-sloping supply curve rather than the perfectly elastic supply of men. If this is the case then, it may pay the employer to split the male and female labor market and offer different wages to the two groups.

The textbook analogy is with third-degree price discrimination in the output market. In this context it may be profitable for a monopolistic pro-ducer to charge different prices to consumers with different elasticities of demand, charging higher prices to those with lowest elasticity. Textbook examples are the discounts offered to students on services such as rail and air travel, newspaper subscriptions, etc. Along the same lines, it is profitable for an employer to price discriminatingly between workers (or groups of them) with different elasticities of supply, paying women less than men if their elasticity is lower. In this case, women are paid less than their marginal value product. Reagan (1978) provides some evidence that female economists in the United States work under monopsonistic conditions. Freeman's (1982) account of working mothers accepting low pay from "understanding employers" could be described alternately as a voluntary acceptance of a compensating differential or as exploitation of a weak bargaining position.

Statistical Discrimination

The theory of "statistical discrimination" provides another explanation of why rational employers with no specific taste for discrimination might in practice discriminate in favor of men (Phelps 1972; Aigner and Cain 1977). Statistical discrimination arises in a world of imperfect information on individual workers' productivity. In this context it may be impossible, or too costly, for employers to obtain sufficient information to estimate precisely the productivity of each prospective worker. They then have to rely on observable personal characteristics, such as education, but to some extent also gender.

A profit-maximizing employer would thus pay men higher wages than women, or would have preferred to hire men, if their expected net productivity was higher. In the case of risk-averse employers, the difference in the expected net productivity of men and women can be due to a variety of factors. The average net productivity of women could be lower than that of men's, for example, because of women's higher turnover costs. The individual variation around the mean could be larger for women than for men because they vary more in their attachment to the labor market. Finally, the signals used by the employer to predict individual workers' productivity, such as interviews and aptitude test scores, may be weaker predictors for women than for men. The extent of statistical discrimination therefore depends on how far men and women differ in their average productivity net of turnover and other costs, and in the differential ability of the two groups to provide signals of comparable strength.

Policy Implications of Different Types of Discrimination

In the view of mainstream economists, not all types of wage differentiation reflect unequal treatment of women in the labor market warranting antidiscrimination intervention. The general view is that "pure discrimination" is a demand-side phenomenon and should not reflect supply-side differences in preferences or in supply elasticity. Monopsonistic discrimination is therefore not real discrimination, and crowding is not discriminatory unless it is generated by demand-side barriers to mobility. Similarly, statistical discrimination is not unfair discrimination: women's lower wages simply reflect their lower expected marginal product, which could be improved by better information. However, taste-based discrimination is not only unfair but inefficient, as it distorts the true relative productivity of men and women.

Why the Low Pay of Women Part-Timers?

As the low pay of part-timers is not a universal phenomenon, but a particular feature of the British scene, there is no general theory from which we can draw a widely accepted explanation. A taste for discrimination seems an improbable explanation for pay gaps between identical women working full- and part-time. It is more likely that statistical discrimination operates, leading employers to underestimate the productivity or motivation of some part-time employees. It seems more likely that labor-market imperfection, including monopsony, and segmentation are the major forces at work. Particularly British factors could be the lack of penetration of part-time jobs by collective agreements, and incentives in the tax and National Insurance contribution structure to keep total earnings below certain thresholds. A possible demand-side explanation for low pay in part-time jobs is that part-timers' productivity per hour employed is lower than full-timers' due to "warm-up" effects. If it take some "dead" time to get going—change into a uniform or get machinery started, for example—employing full-timers could be more effective. On the other hand, full-timers are more likely to use their employer's time for regular work breaks and occasional authorized absences (for example, to see the dentist) than workers employed on shorter shifts. Whatever factors lead to low pay for part-timers, they are likely to overlap strongly with any pay penalties to domestic responsibilities. In the British context at least, these often lead to part-time employment, and most part-time jobs are filled by workers with families. Actual or presumed commitment to paid work may be part of the story (Hakim 1991). Waldfogel (1993, 1995) has already established in a preliminary version of the NCDS data that women who take maternity leave do not appear to suffer the reduced pay observed for other mothers. This work is taken further in chapter 6.

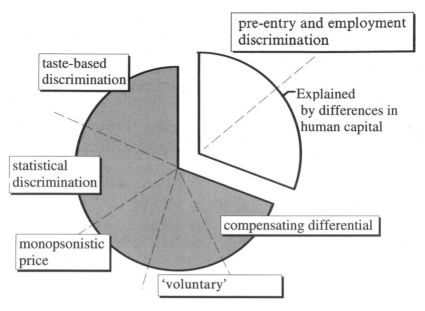

Figure 2.1
Potential components of the pay gap

Sources of Wage Gaps: A Summary

Wage differentials may result from a variety of sources other than the unequal treatment of women in the labor market. These are summarized in
figure 2.1. At least some of the variation in pay results from differences
in productive endowments. This would accord with a competitive labor
market where the wage rate equals the marginal value product of labor.
The unshaded area in the graph, of arbitrary size, represents the relative
share of this component in the total gender differential.

In the view of most, this element of the gender gap is not discriminatory. However, some argue the differential acquisition of human capital
characteristics by men and women to be itself the outcome of discrimination. If so, the unshaded area may include the result of some pre–
labor market and/or employment discrimination.

The darker shade represents the residual wage differential not attributable to differences in endowments. This may reflect one or more of the
following factors: differences in the degree of desirability of the jobs done
by the two groups (compensating wage differentials); systematic gender
differences in preferences for some types of job ("voluntary" crowding); in

the elasticity of supply (monopsonistic price discrimination), in their expected productivity or in intragroup variation in productivity (statistical discrimination). After all these factors are taken into account, there remains the possibility of unequal treatment resulting from a pure "taste for discrimination."

Measuring the Extent of Discrimination

It is evident from chapter 1 that, although the gender gap has obviously narrowed over the last twenty years, earnings differentials between men and women remain a feature of all western industrial countries. Nevertheless, testing whether the source of these differentials is discrimination—taste-based or otherwise—is not straightforward.

How Can the Various Determinants of Unequal Pay Be Decomposed?

The standard econometric method of accounting for the gender wage gap involves estimating separate earnings equations for male and female employees, taking the logarithm of their earnings. One reason to do this is the distribution of earnings is usually skew, tending to approach the lognormal distribution.

These equations are commonly specified thus:

$$\ln w_i^S = \beta^S X_i^S + v_i^S \quad S = m, f \tag{2.1}$$

where i denotes individuals and S indicates the individual's gender, male (m) or female (f), w stands for earnings per hour per employee, X is a matrix of explanatory variables, β is a vector of parameters, and v an error term.[3]

The gross differential is then decomposed according to what is known as the Oaxaca-Blinder procedure (Oaxaca 1973; Blinder 1973), which in the case of the gender gap takes the form

$$\ln w_m - \ln w_f = (\bar{X}_m - \bar{X}_f)\beta_m + (\beta_f - \beta_m)\bar{X}_f, \tag{2.2}$$

where the bar indicates mean values. The formula in (2.2) permits decomposition of the aggregate pay differential into its explained component due to differences in mean characteristics (i.e., the dark shaded area in figure 2.1) and the part due to differences in parameters (i.e., the unshaded area in figure 2.1). Since the gender gap is expressed in terms of logs, the component ratios can simply be added together. This is more convenient than the multiplication required when the wage differential is expressed in levels. Another convenient feature of working in logarithms is that differences in log wages reflect proportional differences in wages, rather than absolute differences, which are not comparable from time to time or place to place.

Oaxaca defined a "discrimination index" D as the weighted difference in parameters expressed as a percentage differential. When the parameter differences are weighted by female characteristics (as they are in (2.2)) the index is known as D_f and is given by

$$D_f = \{\exp[(\beta_m - \beta_f) \cdot \bar{X}_f] - 1\} \cdot 100.^4 \tag{2.3}$$

This reflects the proportionate difference between what the "average woman" (i.e., a hypothetical woman with average X_f characteristics) would earn if paid according to the male pay schedule and what she is actually paid. Similarly the parameter differences may be evaluated as they would be experienced by the "average man" facing women's rates of pay. In this case the parameter differences are weighted by X_m to give

$$D_m = \{\exp[(\beta_m - \beta_f) \cdot \bar{X}_m] - 1\} \cdot 100. \tag{2.4}$$

It is worth noting that some systematic differences in productivity-related characteristics between men and women may be very difficult to quantify and may not be captured by the X's. In this case the dividing line between the explained and the unexplained components of figure 2.1 may not be accurately drawn.

Selection Bias

There is a question of potential bias in the selection of women into the earnings equations, arising from the fact that wages can be observed only for those women who were in employment. These women may be thought of as a self-selected sample. Limiting the analysis exclusively to them could either under- or overestimate the wage opportunities available to all women. The decision by the others not to take paid work may, for example, reflect a lower wage offer. If so, limiting the analysis to those who are in jobs and to wage offers that have been accepted will systematically overestimate the wage opportunities available to the average woman.

It is customary to account for this possible bias in the estimates of women's earnings functions following a two-step procedure suggested by

Heckman (1979). In the basic model there are only two types of women: those in paid work and the others. The first step of this procedure compares women observed with pay with those who are not, and generates a score indicating each woman's probability of being in the waged sample. The second step includes this sample selection score in the analysis of wages. Where more than one type of paid work is allowed for (i.e., full-time and part-time), the selection equation can allow for more than two categories of women by means of an ordered (or multinominal) probit or logit. The equation would then estimate for each individual woman the probabilities of her being in each of the possible forms of paid work. Details of the procedures we have used are found in the appendixes to chapters 4 and 6.

What Should Be Allowed to Vary in the Assessment of Equal Pay?

There is some debate in the literature on the explanatory variables to be included in the earnings equation.[5] There are empirical difficulties in operationalizing the theoretically straightforward principle that discrimination is purely a demand-side phenomenon. This implies that any supply-side variable that may result in differences in wages should enter the earnings equation. This will obviously include personal productivity-related characteristics—such as ability, education, experience, etc.—but also the employee's preferences for the nonpecuniary aspects of the job as well as some measure of his or her elasticity of supply.

Since, however, direct measures of employees' preferences and supply elasticities are rarely available, some analysts propose using employer and job characteristics as proxies for individual differences in tastes and elasticities. Others warn that the crowding of women into some jobs and occupations may reflect discrimination and demand-side barriers to entry in the male-dominated sectors rather than women's choices. They therefore reject the inclusion of such variables among the characteristics from which the explained component is calculated.

In reality, any differences between men and women in occupations and in other job characteristics are likely to reflect both employment discrimination and differences in preferences. Thus the most parsimonious human capital specification of the earnings function could overestimate the extent of gender discrimination by treating all job-related differences as unexplained. On the other hand, a broader specification, with occupational and job-related controls, could underestimate gender discrimination by masking any discriminatory origins of job-related differences (Blau and Ferber 1987).

Brown et al. (1980) and Gill (1994) have attempted to separate the role played by individual choice and employment discrimination in determining gender differences in occupational distribution. They distinguish between the probability that an individual will choose an occupation and the probability that a person will be hired for the desired job. No such attempt is made in this study, but for the 1958 cohort, we do present models that include job characteristics as well as excluding them.

Unpacking Unequal Pay: The Evidence to Date from Britain

A number of studies of gender wage differentials in Britain have taken the Oaxaca-Blinder approach and used human capital earnings functions to decompose the gender gap (Greenhalgh 1980; Zabalza and Arrufat 1985; Dolton and Makepeace 1986; Miller 1987; Joshi and Newell 1989; Wright and Ermisch 1991; Harkness 1996; Blackaby et al. 1997). Difference in education and experience (where known) have been important factors in accounting for wage gaps, even though the human capital gap between the sexes has been falling. Not all of the data sets used have evidence on actual work experience. Zabalza and Arrufat (1985), Miller (1987), and Blackaby et al. (1997) impute an employment record, constructed from information on the number of children. In her analyses of the General Household Survey (GHS) for 1974 and 1983, Harkness (1996), like Greenhalgh (1980), uses age as a proxy for experience. Her data for 1992–93 come from the British Household Panel Study (BHPS), a new source for actual employment history. As far as the genderwise comparison goes, results with and without information on work experience are similar (Wright and Ermisch, Women and Employment Survey; Harkness, BHPS, full-timers). For analyses involving women part-timers, actual experience made more difference in the BHPS. Among full-timers in the GHS, Blackaby and colleagues report that results were similar using either age or imputed experience. This suggests that full-timers' actual experience is more closely correlated with their age as they are less likely than part-timers to have discontinuous careers. Despite the importance of human capital variables in explaining differentials within and between the sexes, most of the studies suggest the persistence of a gap in treatment of equivalent male and female workers, albeit also shrinking, after the introduction of equal pay legislation in the mid-1970s.

In the period before the Equal Pay Act came into force, estimates of Discrimination Indices offered by Greenhalgh (1980) were 24% between single men and women and 46% between married persons (with women's pay as the base). Using an index of discrimination quantifying how much more a woman with average characteristics would be paid if remunerated as a man, Joshi and Newell (1989) estimate D_f among 26-year-olds of all marital status in 1972 at 51 percent. After the implementation of the Equal Pay Act, and the associated rise in women's relative pay, the studies generally indicate lower otherwise unaccounted gender gaps. For 1975, Greenhalgh estimated a 10% premium between single men and women and around 35% for the married. Joshi and Newell's estimated D_f for 32-year-olds in 1977–78 was 32%, and Dolton and Makepeace's estimate for graduates in 1977 was 20%. Zabalza and Arrufat (1985), using data for married couples in 1975, attributed most of the 61% gender gap to home time as they imputed it, leaving an estimated D_f of only 9%. Later evidence suggests that this was suspiciously low. Miller's estimate for married men and women in the 1980 GHS was 14% for the basic human capital model. Wright and Ermisch (1991), using data on married persons from the Women and Employment Survey of 1980, estimate gender discrimination between 22% and 24% (with and without allowance for sample selection).

The human capital model estimated by Harkness (1996) yields the following D_f for full-timers of all ages: 40%, 1973; 27%, 1983; 22%, 1992 (estimates in fuller models are not much different). There was less improvement in the ratio of men's wages to part-timers. Parameter differences here accounted for a premium of 53% in 1973, 52% in 1983, and 40% in 1992. Blackaby et al. (1997) are concerned with the distribution of unequal pay between high and low earnings brackets and with patterns of change over time, from 1973 to 1991. They find that the remuneration gap for full-timers closed more at the top end (ninetieth percentile of the wage distribution) than the bottom. Changes in rates of remuneration occurred more in the early years, while changes in attributes became more of a factor in the 1980s. The key "price change" was in the remuneration of qualifications.

Thus far the attempts to adjust the pay gap for differential attributes suggest that by the time the Equal Pay Act was in force, the pay premium enjoyed by men had already begun to fall, but by most accounts it was far from being eliminated.

The impact of equal pay legislation on *employment* is not the subject of this study. Broadly, there was not the net adverse effect on the number of female jobs that might have been expected from a rise in women's relative wage. Several authors point to strong demand, induced by the changing industrial structure (Zabalza and Tzannatos 1985; Borooah and Lee 1988; Joshi et al. 1985). Manning (1996) suggests that monopsonistic conditions in the labor market for women allowed for an increase in employment at the same time as a wage increase.

Unpacking Unequal Pay: Our Approach

We adopt a rather agnostic position to the various theoretical sources of the gender pay gap. Our point of departure is the analysis of wage differentials in terms of personal characteristics only. This is done in chapter 4 using a set of characteristics available in a comparable form for both the 1946 and the 1958 cohort. The cross-cohort comparison enables us to chart how the various components of wage differentials have changed for employees in their early thirties over the period that equal pay has been in force. We also show a "human capital" equation for the 1958 cohort in chapter 5, slightly extended to include data on employer training and a different measure of employment experience. The focus of chapter 5, however, is on the effect of introducing explanatory variables on employer and job characteristics and occupation. All along human capital and job characteristics—other than the decision to take a part-time or full-time job—are treated as exogenous, that is, not as being chosen by the employee at the same time as the wage is set. Following the discussion of the previous chapter, we expect the parameter component of the differential to decline as we move to more extensive specifications. The more extensive specification will treat the segregation of women in less remunerative jobs as a valid reason for their low pay rather then a route through which discrimination operates.

In line with the more recent work on gender differentials, we distinguish between women employed part-time and those employed full-time, since these two sectors are known to offer different rates of pay to women of equivalent human capital (Ermisch and Wright 1992; Harkness 1996). We compute three indices of unequal treatment in three pay gaps between: (1) men and women in full-time employment; (2) women full-time and part-time; and (3) men full-timers and women part-timers. We also reconstruct the wage differential between men and all women, by taking a weighted sum of (1) and (3).

We also allow for more than one "participation" status in the selection equation. Chapter 4 uses an ordered probit model to calculate the probability of a woman (1) not working; (2) working only part-time; and (3) working full-time. There were no significant selection effects detected in either part-time or full-time employment. Following this, the estimates in chapter 5 are reported without selection adjustment. However, the extent of selectivity picked up by our model increases in chapter 6, where a multinominal logit is used to allow for selectivity into motherhood (and maternity leave) as well as employment status. This serves to remind us that the focus on earnings and human capital is drawing on data from more complex lives than can be captured in the measurable variables included in the model.

In estimating the determinants of earnings we allow for the maximum possible flexibility by running separate earnings equations for the three groups: male full-timers, female full-timers, and female part-timers. This allows for each group's remuneration of a given endowment or a given job characteristic to be different. Where statistical tests indicate that coefficients are similar in two or more equations, we constrain them to be equal (in the interests of parsimony). The most parsimonious model would apply one common set of parameters to a pooled sample, the least would fit three times as many by taking three separate samples. In chapter 5 we arrive at models that are somewhat simplified after some pooling of samples and some discarding of superfluous terms. Chapter 6 concentrates on models for female employees, allowing for possible variation by the presence of children as well as by whether the job is full-time. The objective is to see to what extent women's low pay can be accounted for by their different, if not unequal, domestic responsibilities.

3   Unpacking Unequal Pay: Data Sources

This chapter introduces the main sources of information for our study, two of the three British Birth Cohort Studies. We outline the areas in which these studies have been used in the past and point out why cohort studies are particularly suited to this analysis. The two studies we use are well timed to ascertain the effectiveness of equal opportunity legislation. We then sketch a statistical portrait of the two cohorts, showing changes in education, family formation, and the attachment of women to the labor market that leads to employment and earnings in 1978 and 1991 respectively. The gross gender gaps in earnings that emerge from the cohort studies are compared with averages recorded for the population of all ages in those years. Finally, we give details of the variables used in the following chapters to unpack the components of the gross gap.

The British Birth Cohort Studies

Britain's longitudinal data resources include our internationally unique set of prospective surveys that have followed three groups of individuals from birth into adulthood. Each of the birth cohort studies has nationwide coverage, and each began as a perinatal study of all births in one week. None was initiated with the intention, or at least firm plans, to do a longitudinal study. Their general structure is described in figure 3.1.

The original study, in 1946, was conducted jointly by the Royal College of Gynaecologists and Obstetricians and the Population Investigation Committee. It was a response to concern about the standard of maternity services and low fertility (Joint Committee 1948). A tight budget, in time and cash, dictated that a week's births be studied rather than a sample spread over a year. The study week (March 3–9, 1946) was chosen as the first available (Douglas 1976).

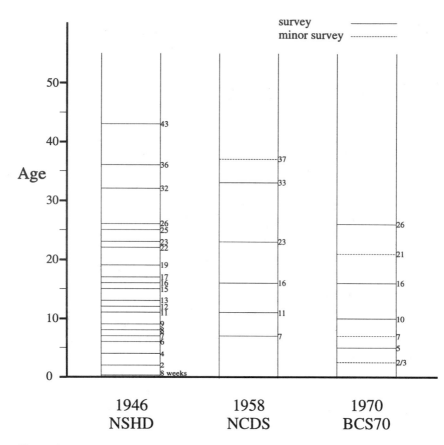

Figure 3.1
British Longitudinal Birth Cohort Studies
Source: Adapted and updated from Ekinsmyth 1996 and Wadsworth et al. 1984.

There were 16,695 births in England, Scotland, and Wales that week, and data were collected for 13,687 of them. Part of the shortfall was due to a few local authorities not participating (7%). When it was decided to follow up these births at age 2, practical and cost considerations again constrained the design, setting a reduced size of the sample to follow up. The relatively small numbers of children whose father was in a nonmanual (or agricultural labor) occupation were all retained in the stratified sample. Of the rest, with urban working-class fathers, a sample of one in four was followed up. Illegitimate births (672) and multiple births (180) were deliberately set aside. The former had almost all been adopted and would have been difficult to follow; the twins were thought to be too few to analyze.

Table 3.1
The MRC National Survey of Health and Development (dates and types of data collection)

Year	Age in years	Data collector	Number contacted	Percentage contacted
1948	2	HV	4,689	94
1950	4	HV	4,700	96
1952	6	SD; SN or HV	4,603	95
1953	7	SN or HV; SD; T	4,480	93
1954	8	SN or HV; T	4,435	92
1955	9	SN or HV	4,181	87
1956	10	T	4,077	85
1957	11	SN or HV; SD; T	4,281	89
1959	13	T	4,127	86
1961	15	SN or HV; T; SD	4,274	89
1965	19	HV	3,561	75
1966	20	P	3,899	83
1968	22	P	3,885	84
1969	23	P	3,026	67
1971	25	P	3,307	74
1972	26	I	3,750	85
1978	32	P	3,340	78
1982	36	RN	3,322	86
1989	43	RN	3,262	85

Source: Wadsworth 1991.
Notes:
HV = health visitor; SN = school nurse; SD = school doctor; T = teacher; P = postal contact;
I = interviewer; RN = research nurse.

The follow-up sample of the National Survey of Health and Development therefore starts at age 2 in 1948, with 5,362 cases of legitimate singleton births. This is one-third of the original births. To be representative of the class origins of the cohort, the data need to be reweighted.[1] Readers will note where we report reweighted data in the following chapters.

Once the NSHD study was under way it involved a number of further collections of data, frequent during childhood and less so in adulthood. In childhood, the data were collected from the mothers by health visitors and also from teachers, school medical officers, and administration of tests at school. In adulthood, data was collected by interviews with the cohort members at ages 26, 36, and 43 and by postal questionnaires at other points (see table 3.1). We make particular use here of the postal survey sent

out in December 1977 and returned as the cohort members approached
their 32nd birthday. Further data collection is planned at age 53 in 1999.

For thirty-three years, the 1946 study was directed by Dr. James
Douglas, with whom the study became identified. It is now officially the
MRC National Survey of Health and Development, to reflect its funding
by the Medical Research Council. It is based at University College Medical
School in London under the direction of Professor Michael Wadsworth.
We name the study "MRC" for short to distinguish it from the NCDS.[2]

The next two cohorts, the 1958 National Child Development Study
(NCDS) and the 1970 British Cohort Study (BCS70) also started as perinatal studies, becoming follow-up studies as the necessary resources were
secured. NCDS was founded by the National Birthday Trust in 1958.
Childhood follow-ups also involved the family, school, and medical services as informants. In contrast to the 1946 study, these contacts were
less frequent, but they did attempt to follow the whole cohort (see table
3.2), taking subsamples only on occasions, as illustrated in figure 3.1. The
most recent contact with NCDS members, at age 37, is for a 10% sample

Table 3.2
The National Child Development Study: Dates and types of data collection

Survey Year	PMS (1958)	NCDS1 (1965)	NCDS2 (1969)	NCDS3 (1974)	EXAM (1978)	NCDS4 (1981)	NCDS5 (1991)
Age	Birth	7	11	16	20	23	33
a	17,733	16,883	16,835	16,915	16,906	16,457	15,600
	Mother	Parents	Parents	Parents			
		School	School	School	School		
		Tests	Tests	Tests			
	Medical	Medical	Medical	Medical			
		Subject	Subject	Subject		Subject	Subject
				Census			Census
							Spouse/Partner
							Mother[c]
							Children
b	17,414	15,468	15,503	14,761	14,370	12,537	11,407
d	98%	92%	92%	87%	85%	76%	73%

Note: MRC percentages are weighted, sample numbers are not.
a. Target sample—immigrants with appropriate date of birth included for NCDS1–3.
b. Achieved sample—at least one survey instrument partially completed.
c. This could be the cohort member, their spouse, or partner.
d. Response rate from target sample.

only, intended particularly to assess basic skills at literacy and numeracy. We do not use these data here.

The members of the 1958 cohort have been contacted in two full sweeps as adults, age 23 in 1981 and age 33 in 1991, the main source of information for this study. The first full sweep in adult life for the 1970 cohort took place by means of a postal survey in 1996, whose analysis is just beginning (Bynner and Ferri 1997). Both the NCDS and the 1970 cohort studies have had a checkered funding and management history, but both studies are now housed at the Social Statistics Research Unit at City University, under the direction of Professor John Bynner and Peter Shepherd.[3] (The data are available through the ESRC Data Archive.) The ESRC has also played a major role in funding recent data collection, and it is hoped that funding arrangements are being established to ensure the continuation of the follow-ups. Cofunders (with the ESRC) for the 1991 NCDS5 sweep included the U.S. National Institute for Child Health and Development (NICHD) for the interview with NCDS cohort members' children and their mother. The NCDS therefore has, like the MRC study, a follow-through to the second generation, though neither is shown in figure 3.1. In the case of NCDS, the data collection was designed to be parallel, with similar mother-and-child data collected in the U.S. National Longitudinal Survey of Youth, NLSY. The U.S. study has much in common with NCDS. Its members are a cohort born over a period that includes 1958, but that spans 7 years. They were followed from ages 14 to 21 starting in 1979, not from birth. There is also a parallel in the United States to the 1946 cohort in the National Longitudinal Survey of Young Women (NLS-YW), which follows a group of women who were aged 14 to 24 when first interviewed in 1968. Their birth years span 1944 to 1954.

Previous Uses of the British Birth Cohorts

The diversity of types of information about the cohort members' unfolding lives and dates upon which it has been gathered yields great potential for a wide range of research. Seldom have the antecedents and consequences of so many types of events or states been linked. The main use to which the 1946 cohort has been put is to trace into adulthood the health consequences of childhood circumstances and health conditions (Wadsworth 1991; Kuh et al. 1997; Kuh and Ben-Shlomo 1997).

The survey has also been used to study, for example, the adult outcomes of children whose parents divorce (Maclean and Wadsworth 1988,

Wadsworth et al. 1991), and demographic processes such as the timing of family formation (Kiernan 1986; Kiernan and Diamond 1983) and birth intervals (Ní Bhrolcháin 1986). Other labor-related analyses include the occupational psychology studies of Cherry (1984a,b) and studies of employment after childbearing by Joshi and Newell (1987) and Joshi and Hinde (1993).[4] Earnings differentials have been studied by Kuh et al. (1997) with data from age forty-three, and to ages 26 and 32 by Joshi and Newell (1989). All of these topics have been, or could be, studied in the following cohorts (Power et al. 1991; Thompson et al. 1995; Kiernan 1992; and Ferri 1993).

NCDS is even more of a multipurpose study than the MRC cohort. There have been more studies on NCDS data concerned with employment matters. Some relevant examples include Bynner et al. (1996), who use data on self-perceived skills that are not brought into the present study. Macran et al. (1996) explore the employment histories of women across childbearing and compare them with the experience of women born in 1946. Joshi et al. (1995) and Joshi and Davies (1996) look at the contributions women's earnings make to family incomes in the 1958 cohort. They conclude that few attain the financial independence to which most of the cohort seem to aspire. The child-care arrangements, many informal, made by NCDS women at age 33 are described in detail by Ward et al. (1996). Occupational attainments have been studied by Harper and Haq (1995). Intergenerational continuities in income have been studied at the Institute for Fiscal Studies (Johnson and Reed 1996). A complete list of NCDS publications and questionnaires are available from SSRU (NCDS User Support Group 1995).

The British Birth Cohort Studies as Evidence for the Analysis of Earnings Differentials

The major advantage of the cohort studies in an analysis of earnings differentials is that they provide, alongside adult earnings, information on individual education and work histories, as well family background and a measure from childhood of innate ability. An additional advantage of using these two studies is their high degree of comparability, which allows cross-cohort, as well as intra-cohort, analysis. Moreover, the timing of the relevant sweeps of the two cohorts makes them particularly suited to analyze the effect of equal pay legislation on the gender pay gap. However, follow-up studies have their own problems.

The Advantages of Intra-cohort Analysis

The review in chapter 2 of the theory of discrimination and of the empirical debate about measuring it points toward individual and job characteristics as determinants of any nondiscriminatory pay gap across gender. Any empirical attempt to measure discrimination therefore needs to measure gender differences in human capital attributes and job characteristics.

Among the relevant human capital variables are the individual's ability, his or her level of education, the extent of training undertaken (whether general or "on-the-job"), total employment experience, and the length of service with the same employer. Detailed information on these variables, however, is very rarely available. Most previous studies in the area have been forced either to ignore their effects (as for the training and tenure variables) or use proxies (with potential experience often used in place of actual experience).

These solutions are not satisfactory. There are wide gender differences in the proportion of employees receiving training and in the length of service. Women often experience lengthy career interruptions. An additional limitation of other data sets used in the literature is that they rarely combine information on personal and job characteristics. Such a combination is needed to investigate the role played by differences in preferences or labor-market segregation in the gender pay gap.

The Advantages of Cross-cohort Analysis

Each cohort study offers the possibility of tracing sequences within individual lifetimes. Single cohort studies, however, have the disadvantage that they represent no one other than themselves passing through a particular point of the life cycle at a particular historical moment. Life-cycle effects are confounded with period effects. The existence of comparator cohorts overcomes this drawback, providing evidence on the same part of the life course at different historical periods. The effect of changes in historical circumstances on life-cycle processes can be investigated. Cross-cohort studies reap the full advantage of cohort-study data. This is one of the first to use both NCDS data from age 33 and MRC data at a comparable age. The wage data we analyze for the 1946 sweep were collected by a postal questionnaire mailed out in December 1977. This was returned, mostly over the next few months, as members of the cohort approached their 32nd birthday in March 1978.

The Importance of the Timing of the Two Studies

The timing of the relevant sweeps of the two cohorts makes them well suited to the intertemporal analysis of the gender gap. The MRC provides evidence on pay and employment history around the beginning of 1978. As we saw in chapter 1, by that time the Equal Pay Act appears to have achieved most of its initial impact. Table 3.5 shows that, among 32-year-olds the crude excess of male hourly wages over all female employees was 60%, at the logarithmic mean. By 1991, the gap among employees born in 1958 had fallen to 47%.

One may be tempted to interpret this decrease as further success of the antidiscrimination policies described in chapter 1—the implementation and strengthening of equal pay and equal opportunity legislation. However, the 1980s also saw a marked convergence in the productive endowments held by men and women. The NCDS cohort members, especially if women, tend to have higher levels of human capital that the members of the earlier cohort.

Problems with Follow-up Data

One drawback of using follow-up studies is the problem of keeping track of everyone. As the survey loses contact with cohort members, it is said to suffer from attrition. If the probability of attrition is systematically related to a given personal characteristic—for example, being male or poorly educated—there is attrition bias. All the cohort studies attempt to maintain contact by sending an annual birthday card. As can be seen from table 3.1, the MRC Study has maintained contact with well over 80% of its subjects who were "available" at each of its interview sweeps. The postal sweep of 1978, which we use, netted somewhat fewer (78%). The target population is defined as those who were alive, living in Britain, and not having made a permanent refusal. In 1978, 306 cohort members had died, 605 were abroad, and 158 had permanently refused. Since the age 26 interview, 310 had been lost (more male than female). Tests reported in Joshi and Newell (1989) and Timæus and Joshi (1983) suggested that there was not much systematic selection of respondents. Cases lost between twenty-six and thirty-two were not seriously biased. For a more complete study of response bias in the MRC Study, see Wadsworth (1991).

The NCDS target sample, shown in table 3.2, includes immigrants to Britain with the relevant birth dates, recruited into the sample while they were at school. The response rate shown here makes no adjustment for permanent refusals. With over three times the numbers to contact than the MRC Study, the response rate of 73% for 1991 also seems respectable, but this is only one, rather generous definition of response.

More than 17,000 people have at some stage been in contact with NCDS, of whom 11,407 took part in the 1991 interview (NCDS5). The numbers of cases with complete information on all instruments in NCDS5, let alone all previous sweeps, is considerably smaller. This does not greatly bias the results on employees, however, though we are aware that the least able cohort members were least likely to respond at all to the follow-up (Shepherd 1993).

Another caveat about these two birth cohort studies is that they are not a reliable source of data on ethnicity. The MRC Study drew its sample before there was a significant number of nonwhite people being born in Britain. The NCDS, given its attempt to recruit immigrants, ought to have more representative coverage. However, ethnic minorities are among those for whom follow-up was least successful (Shepherd 1993). Thus we have not included race in our models of earnings, nor attempted to measure race discrimination. Other data suggest this is also a problem in the British labor market (Blackaby et al. 1994; Equal Opportunities Commission 1994).

A Statistical Portrait of the Two Cohorts

Although born only 12 years apart, by their early thirties the two cohorts were considerably different in terms of the human capital they had acquired and the employment and family status they had reached. Table 3.3 shows that the educational attainments of both sexes had risen, women's more so. Those with higher educational qualifications accounted for 21% of men and 10% of women in the MRC cohort, rising to 27% of men and 25% of women in NCDS. Correspondingly, the proportions with no qualifications had come down. This reflects a substantial increase in the schooling of adolescents between the early 1960s and the 1970s. For the 1946 cohort the minimum school leaving age was 15, for NCDS members, 16.

Among the various transitions to adulthood over the next 16 or so years, let us look first at family formation. The later cohort delayed childbearing. By age 26, 72% of the women born in 1946 had had a child, compared to only 50% of those in NCDS. By age 32, 87% of the MRC women (and 72% of the men) were parents, but at age 33 in NCDS, 25%

Table 3.3
Educational attainments of men and women in two birth cohorts (percentages)

	MRC (1946)		NCDS (1958)	
Highest qualification	Men	Women	Men	Women
None	46	45	11	14
Some	7	11	16	19
O-level	14	25	26	35
A-level	13	9	19	8
Higher nondegree	11	7	13	14
Degree	10	3	14	11
Sample size	1,603	1,605	5,495	5,647

of women and 41% of men had not (yet) had children. Indeed the postponement of childbearing may have become indefinite in a larger number of cases (Kiernan 1997; Macran et al. 1996).

Women's Employment Participation over the Life Course by Cohort Born since 1930

For men the transition to labor-force membership was fairly universal by the mid-twenties. However, patterns of participation in the labor force for women are more complicated, and inextricably connected to the delay in childbearing noted above. They are also part of a general upward trend toward women's greater participation in the labor market, as shown in figure 1.1 and table 1.1. Women's participation in paid work has been increasing at most ages and in all countries at a time when the men's has tended to fall. The feminization of employment is a general phenomenon, not limited to our cohorts or to the age groups they represent. How do these cohorts fit into the broader trends in female labor-force participation?

To some extent the phenomenon is age and cohort specific. In Britain in particular, the trend initially took the form of successive generations being more likely to participate on a part-time basis in midlife, after returning to the labor force from a break for childbearing. At the same time, the propensity to be employed full-time fell over the twenties and then remained basically constant over midlife ages. This was the longitudinal perspective on the dipping age-participation profile recorded in the 1980 Women and Employment Survey (illustrated in OECD 1988).

Figure 3.2 tracks the participation of five-year birth cohorts of women up to 1994 using data collected (mostly retrospectively) by the British

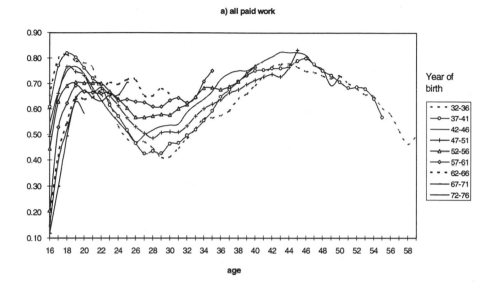

a) all paid work

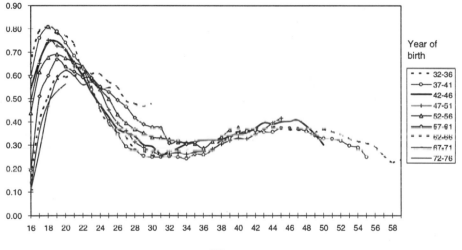

b) full-time employment

Figure 3.2
Women's participation in paid work
Source: British Household Panel Study.

Household Panel Survey (BHPS). The cohorts born since World War II show an increasing propensity to be in employment at age 25 and above. This contrasts with the tendency for participation of the earlier cohorts to fan out after age 30. However, it mirrors earlier trends in Sweden, the United States, and France (OECD 1988).

Before age 25, the more recent, postwar cohorts have lower employment participation, reflecting their increased educational enrolment. They also show increased full-time participation at ages 24–30 (see figure 3.2, part (b)) and a rising propensity of older women to be employed part-time.

The MRC cohort of 1946 passed through their late twenties too soon to be caught up in the rise in full-time employment at these ages that occurred in the 1980s. They were just embarking on their "return to the labor market" phase when sampled at age 32. Many of those then sampled had been out of employment for some years during their twenties. Figure 3.2 suggests that their employment in part-time work would have continued to rise sharply after this study loses track of them. Although full-time participation would have increased less, overall participation would have peaked at around 80% in their early forties.

The NCDS 1958 cohort is among the 1957–61 group shown in figure 3.2. They experience a flatter profile over ages 24 to 33 with an increased propensity to full-time employment. A few BHPS observations for this group beyond age 33 suggest the existence of an additional wave of returnees about to rejoin the labor market at the time the NCDS are interviewed in 1991. Our two cohorts, at 32/33 are contrasted: one is dominated by returnees working part-time, as were the working women of that age in previous generations; the second cohort adds a greater element of full-time employment, often uninterrupted.

At age 26, when the MRC cohort was interviewed in 1972, 44% of women were working outside the home, and 11% part-time. Among their successors, at the same age in 1984, participation rates had increased to 59%, but still just 11% of these women were working part-time.[5] By age 33 the 1958 women not only had considerably higher participation rates in full-time work than the 1946 cohort (as shown in table 3.4), but they had also accumulated more previous employment experience. This result is linked to the postponement of motherhood outlined above, but this is not the full story. The employment of mothers of young children also became more common in NCDS (see chapter 6 and Macran et al. 1996). Continuous employment over the childbearing years became more feasible after the introduction of statutory maternity leave in 1976, too late for the first maternities of most of the 1946 cohort.

Table 3.4
Employment status of two cohorts at two dates (percentages)

	MRC[a]	NCDS
Age 26		
Men		
Full-time	94.1	84.8
Part-time	0.2	0.8
All employed[b]	94.3	85.6
Unemployed	n/a	4.4
Women		
Full-time	32.6	41.2
Part-time	11.1	10.6
All employed[b]	43.6	58.8
Unemployed	n/a	2.0
Age 32/33		
Men		
Full-time	94.7	91.4
Part-time	0.2	0.9
All employed[b]	94.9	93.3
Unemployed	4.1	3.7
Women		
Full-time	23.1	41.5
Part-time	30.7	33.6
All employed[b]	53.8	75.4
Unemployed	1.2	1.1

Notes:
a. MRC values are weighted.
b. The difference between the numbers of "all employed" and the total of part-timers and full-timers reflects the number of cohort members with unknown hours.

Current Employment and Wages

Information on economic activity in 1978 and 1991 is also summarized in table 3.4. This reports the participation rates in each employment status for men and women of both cohorts at ages 26 and 32/33. The rates are defined as a percentage of cohort members with valid information for employment status.

As mentioned above, women from the later cohort are more likely to participate in the labor market at both dates than their counterparts in the earlier cohort. They are also far more likely to be working full-time. Thirty-three-year-old men in the later cohort experience more unemployment than their predecessors, and more than women. There was also more self-employment among men in 1991 (18% of full-timers) than in the MRC cohort in 1978 and than among women (NCDS 7%, MRC 5%). Thus a larger proportion of male than female workers falls outside the purview of waged labor, and hence our analysis. There are also too few men in part-time jobs (one in MRC and 31 in NCDS) for them to be analyzed separately.

The proportion of employees in manual jobs was higher for men than for women, but it fell for both sexes between 1978 and 1991. In the earlier year 54% of the men and 38% of the women were in manual jobs. In 1991 the proportions had dropped to 46% for men, but only 16% for women. Most of the men's manual jobs were classified as skilled. Women's jobs, particularly if part-time, concentrated in junior nonmanual jobs in offices and shops. Among women full-timers there was a higher proportion in professional and intermediate occupations (50% in 1991) than men (46%). The low occupational status of part-time jobs is not unique to these cohorts. However, the high profile of the 33-year-old full-timers is specific to the most recent generations; it was not so apparent in the MRC cohort. In that cohort there are signs of downward mobility among the "returning" women. This contrasts with the net upward mobility experienced by men between ages 26 and 32 (Joshi and Newell 1989; Joshi and Hinde 1993).[6]

Evidence on wages is reported in table 3.5. The age at which earlier wages are available differs across cohorts. It is 23 for NCDS, in 1981, and 26 for the 1946 MRC cohort in 1972. The gender pay gap experienced

Table 3.5
Trends in men's and women's wages in the two cohorts[a]

	Men		All women		
	£ per hour	n	£ per hour	n	Men/Women
MRC[b]					
1972	0.83	1,618	0.52	774	160%
1978	1.95	1,323	1.22	653	160%
NCDS					
1981	2.56	3,502	2.18	3,070	117%
1991	6.80	4,077	4.63	4,024	147%

Notes: the samples cover all cases where pay and hours were reported, irrespective of current employee status.
a. Wages at geometric mean.
b. MRC values are weighted.

by MRC employees did not change between the 1972 and 1978 sweeps. This may be surprising considering that during this period the Equal Pay Act came into force. It is worth noting, however, that the women employed in 1978 were predominantly reentrants into the labor market. They were largely different individuals from those reporting wages in 1972.

By contrast, the 1958 cohort experienced a very sharp divergence of men's and women's pay between 1981 and 1991. The gender gap (defined as a percentage of women's pay) more than doubled, rising from 17% to 47%. This is likely to reflect the differential effect of parenthood on the accumulation of human capital, which derives from women's employment interruptions around childbearing. It may, however, also result from gender discrimination in promotion and career opportunities past the "port-of-entry." We investigate the relative importance of these factors in the following chapters. For the earlier cohort, wage growth was sharply affected by a period effect, masking any life-cycle tendency toward a growing gender gap. This is more apparent in the trajectory of wages in the 1958 cohort.

Our analyses of the two at a roughly fixed point in the life cycle can help to disentangle cohort and period effects. The relatively higher level of education attained by the NCDS women, the increasing proportion of them that followed uninterrupted careers, and the shortening of career breaks are arguably cohort effects, characteristics of a generation. The impact of legislation on unequal treatment is more of a period phenomenon that affected other age groups as well.

In his or her early thirties, the median MRC employee earned hourly earnings in 1978 of £1.95 for men, £1.47 for women full-timers, and £1.05 for women part-timers. On average men were paid 33% more than women employed full-time, and they in turn received 40% more than those working part-time. With the intervening inflation, the rates of pay had risen to £6.80, £5.30, and £3.67 respectively by 1991. The gender gap among full-timers had declined to 28%, but the pay gap between women working full-time and those working part-time had increased by four percentage points, to 44%.

Wage Gaps in the Cohort Studies Compared to Other Sources

An additional limitation of cohort studies is that they refer to a particular age group. Results of their analysis may not apply to other ages. To address this potential problem, figure 3.3 compares the wage ratios for

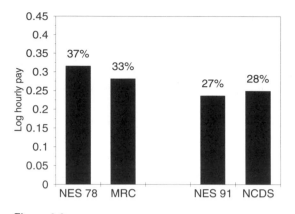

Figure 3.3
Wage gaps: men and women full-timers
Source: Cohort Studies and New Earnings Survey.

full-time employees of all ages (at the median) form the New Earnings Survey (NES) with those from the two cohort studies on employees of a very narrow age band (within one week). The ratios for each date are fairly close, suggesting that the experience of the cohorts has something in common with a wider age group. For 1978, the cohort estimate of 33% is only four points off the NES (37%) value of the log wage gap for full-timers of all ages as used by Harkness (1996). The values of 37% in the 1983 GHS (0.318 in log wages) and 25% in the 1992–93 BHPS (0.221 in log wages) are also close to the NES estimates. All three sources broadly agree on the fact that the gap has closed, but it seems to have closed faster for full-time workers in their thirties. By 1991 the estimate, of 28% for 33-year-olds, is very close to the NES all-age median (27%).

By contrast, in figure 3.4 the two sources agree on the widening of the gap between part-time and full-time workers. The NES puts the increase at 18 percentage points. These particular subsets of the cohort samples put it at only 4. The NES estimate of the differential is at both points smaller than the cohort studies. This can be in part attributed to the poor coverage of the lowest-paid part-timers in the NES. It may also reflect, however, the special characteristics of the 33-year-old compared to all other women in the labor force. This is supported by the fact that the estimated full-time/part-time gaps reported by Harkness are, latterly, even lower: 21% in the 1983 GHS and 23% in the 1992–93 BHPS.

We now turn to other information about the cohort members that may explain why wages are particularly polarized among 33-year-old women and also why pay differs between 33-year-olds of different sexes.

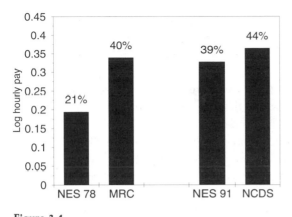
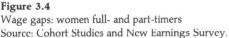

Figure 3.4
Wage gaps: women full- and part-timers
Source: Cohort Studies and New Earnings Survey.

Regression Samples and Variable Definitions

The focus of this analysis is on employees, of whom NCDS included 7,574 (4,083 men and 3,491 women) and the MRC study 2,087 (1,385 men and 702 women). Our earnings functions were estimated from among all cohort members who declared themselves to be currently working as employees and had valid information on wages: 6,800 in NCDS, and 1,790 in the MRC study. Among men, only those working full-time are considered, as so few worked part-time (see table 3.4).

The number of cases with missing values for any of the variables is considerable in both cohorts. Thus selection of samples for regression with complete data leads to another, rather severe form of sample attrition. In chapter 5, we adopt the conventional listwise deletion and end up with little more than 3,000 cases from NCDS to analyze (3,167). In chapters 4 and 6 we do not need the industry variable and we adopt alternative strategies to impute missing values, which preserve larger samples. Definitions of the variables used in the regressions are given in appendix 3.1.

Indeed it is somewhat ironic that, although the cohort studies are particularly suited to the analyses of wages because of the rich information they contain, much of this information was not in a readily usable form. As pioneers in this new material, we had to put considerable effort into checking and cleaning the NCDS5 data, which had only been through limited checks by the time our project started. Much effort had also already been put into the MRC employment data at the London School of Hygiene and Tropical Medicine (see Joshi and Newell 1989). Details of our work on NCDS are given in Paci 1997 and summarized in appendix 3.2.

As shown in appendix 3.1, we use a common set of regressors to predict wages in the cohorts (where they are compared in chapters 4 and 6), which somewhat restricts the models we can specify.[7] In these models we are able to augment the standard earnings equation fitted to cross-sectional data with information on employment history, and with a measure of general ability taken from a test when the cohort members were aged 11 (as described in Douglas 1964). We have by no means fully explored the interrelations between childhood health and home circumstances, and subsequent labor market career. It is our impression that the consequences of family disruption and poor health in childhood on adult achievements are mainly mediated through educational attainments, for which our models do control. The topic of adult health as human capital is the subject of a subsequent project.[8]

The dependent variable in the earnings equation is the log of the gross hourly wage earned in a typical week by the cohort member. This is derived by dividing the wage per period reported (e.g., week, month, year) by the number of hours worked in that period (including overtime). Whatever the payment system actually in place, we convert it to a price per hour using available data on hours worked and total earnings. We may not observe whether hours worked and total earnings. We may not observe whether hours worked exceed the contractual number, nor if workers are paid at an overtime rate. In some professions no contractual hours are specified by employers. This may or may not preclude survey members accurately reporting the hours worked per week. In practice most of the cohort members are likely to have been paid for their time rather than results. The New Earnings Survey shows that in the 1991, the vast majority of payments to employees (89%) are neither payments by results nor attracting shift or overtime premia. Such payments are rare for women and nonmanual male employees, who form the major part of our sample. Our treatment of all employee remuneration as a reward for the reported time involved is a simplification, but it may not be grossly inappropriate.

Having assembled our material and the theoretical and methodological tools, we move on in the following chapters to our investigation of the sources of wage differentials.

4

Is Unequal Treatment a Thing of the Past?*

How far did the equal opportunity legislation of the 1970s result in a reduction in the average pay penalty to being a woman over the 1980s? Were the changes in the treatment of women over the period equally spread across the labor market?

This chapter uses data from both the MRC and the NCDS surveys to address these questions. The emphasis is on human capital, rather than occupational characteristics, which are taken up in the next chapter. We compare the hourly pay of three groups of employees: men employed full-time, women employed full-time, and women employed part-time.

The chapter opens with some elaboration of the exposition on methods specific to this chapter, and not already covered in chapter 2. The first estimates of earnings equations are reported. They are applied first to accounting for wage gaps between average workers. Second, the models are used to investigate the distribution of differential treatment across women.

Method and Variable Definition

To unpack the components of the gender pay gap, we extend the standard Oaxaca-Blinder procedure described in chapter 2. For each cohort we estimate separate earnings equations for men and women working full-time and for female part-time workers. We then test whether the rewards to productivity related characteristics differ across our three groups and whether they change as we move from one cohort to another, so as to change the resulting measure of discrimination. For a full explanation of these tests, see Makepeace et al. (1997).

---

* Gerald Makepeace is a co-author of this chapter.

The model for male full-time employees comprises an earnings equation for each data set of the type

$$\ln w_t^m = \alpha_t^m + \beta_t^m \cdot X^m + u_t^m, \tag{4.1}$$

where w is earnings per hour per employee, t is an index for the cohort with $t = \text{MRC, NCDS}$, m indicates the model for men, α is a constant and X is a vector of characteristics with coefficient vector β. If the coefficient vector, say β^m, were the same for men in both cohorts (i.e., $\beta_{MRC}^m = \beta_{NCDS}^m$), the remuneration of each labor characteristic would appear to be unchanged over time. Then any growth in earnings between the two cohorts for given characteristics would be due to a simple increase in the intercept. Given the growth in money wages between 1978 and 1991, one would expect such a shift even if no other parameters have changed.

The earnings equations for women are not identical to men's because we allow for the possibility of selection bias, as explained in chapter 2. We follow a Heckman procedure extended to allow for two possible employment categories: full-time and part-time. The participation decision is thus given by the ordered probit model described in appendix 4:

$$\ln w_t^k = \alpha_t^k + \beta_t^k \cdot X_t^k + g \cdot \lambda^k + u_t^k, \tag{4.2}$$

where k refers to either full-time or part-time employment. Comparing (4.1) with (4.2), the additional selection term λ^k is designed to investigate the extent of the selectivity bias into full-time and part-time work, which derives from the selection of women into particular work regimes.[1] The selection term has the standard interpretation as the inverse Mill's ratio into each employment category (see appendix 4).

As we move from MRC to NCDS, the selection equations and earnings equations can both change. For instance, the effects of young children on participation could change because of different attitudes to mothers' employment or better support for it. In the wage equation, the return to schooling might change between cohorts, with increasing proportions acquiring qualifications. We therefore estimate the participation equation and the two earnings equations separately for each cohort and then test whether they have the same parameters for the two cohorts.

The specification of the earnings equation is based on a pure human capital model where the only determinants of differences in wages are variations in workers' specific human capital characteristics. Cases have been deleted if they have missing data on any variable other than ability and region.[2] The MRC cohort has 1,583 cohort members with sufficient information to enter the wage regressions: 1,051 men, 263 women working full-time, and 269 women part-timers. The NCDS sample is larger. It includes 5,369 employees: 3,098 men, 1,421 female full-timers, and 850 female part-timers.

The strategy was to find a parsimonious specification in terms of variables and then to test for structural differences between the MRC and NCDS cohorts. Since we are focusing on the differences between the two cohorts and wish to have comparable specifications, the parsimonious specification includes any variable with a coefficient (on either its level or its interaction) significant at 10%. These include:

• *ability:* general ability score from a test at age 11 and a variable indicating a missing value for this score[3];

• *education:* the five dummies specified in table A3.1;

• *experience and job tenure:* years of work experience between the ages 18 and 26, years of work experience between the ages 26 and 32 or 33, years of work experience with current employer, and an interaction between early experience and a dummy for educational qualification higher than or equal to A-levels[4];

• *others:* region of interview and the sample selection term, lambda.[5]

In comparing the characteristics of employees from NCDS with those from MRC, the most striking difference between the cohorts is in the overall improvement, as we have already seen in chapter 3 for the whole cohort, in educational achievements, particularly among women in full-time jobs. Among the employees who entered our earnings equation for the 1946 cohort, only 8% of the women working full-time and 2% of those working part-time held a university degree (as compared to 10% of men); 9% of full-timers and 3% of part-timers held other higher qualifications (as compared to 13% of men). The NCDS cohort women working full-time, however, were more likely than their male counterparts to have higher qualifications (17% of them had a degree and 19% had higher nondegree qualifications, versus values of 15% and 16% for men). NCDS women employed part-time in 1991 have a lower level of qualifications than full-timers, with 7% and 16% having graduate or higher nondegree qualifications respectively—still an improvement on the MRC cohort, where only 5% of part-timers had either qualification.

There is also an important change in male/female differential in work experience and job tenure. The most clearly identifiable trend is an increase in both experience and job tenure among women working full-time— averaging about 1.5 years more over equivalent ages. The apparent shift of the sample away from the Southeast may be no more than an artefact of incomplete coding of region in NCDS.

The table in appendix 4 provides details of the explanatory variables in the participation, or selection, equation for women. These include most of the variables affecting offered wages (except job tenure), along with standard variables thought to affect the woman's reservation wage. The propensity to work is assumed to be a function of variables measuring:

• *family responsibilities:* ever married, number of children, age of youngest child;

• *ability:* defined as above;

• *education:* defined as above;

• *job experience:* years of work experience between the ages 26 and 32; and

• *proxies of alternative income and wealth:* nonworking income, housing tenure, and three dummies reflecting the age at which the husband left school.

Regressions of Participation and Pay: The Results

Table 4.1 reports the analysis of women's participation by ordered probit. Tables 4.2, 4.3, and 4.4 report the estimates of the earnings equations for women working part-time and full-time and for men full-timers.

Participation

First we consider the determinants of women's participation. In a model pooling observations for both cohorts, the ordered probit estimates are largely as expected. There was a general upward shift between cohorts. Among the 1946 cohort, whose coefficients can be read off the first column of table 4.1, the probability of women participating, and participating full-time, is reduced by marriage: for both cohorts it is reduced by having children, but it increases with the age of the youngest. Ability and educational attainments have significant and positive effects on participation for both cohorts, and so does having a husband who left school before 17 years of age. Being an owner-occupier reduces participation among the earlier cohort, although nonlabor income appears to increase it, possibly reflecting the low participation rates of wives of men with no earnings, and the general weakening of income effects since the 1950s (Joshi and Hinde 1993).

Table 4.1
Ordered probit maximum likelihood estimates

	All women		If NCDS	
	Coefficient	*t*-ratio	Coefficient	*t*-ratio
Constant	−0.732	5.37	0.924	4.05
Human capital				
Ability at 11	0.008	3.72	−0.007	2.14
O-levels	0.134	2.99	−0.135	1.63
Work experience, 26−32	0.317	31.52	−0.124	6.21
Husband's education				
O-levels	0.504	6.48	−0.422	3.38
A-levels	0.146	1.78	−0.081	0.52
Further and higher	0.454	1.99	−0.460	1.77
Alternative income and wealth				
Nonworking income	0.464	2.19	−0.530	2.32
Owner-occupier	−0.263	6.58	0.295	3.26
Family commitments				
Ever married	−1.176	8.64	1.068	7.63
Youngest child <5	−0.155	1.64	−0.767	7.01
Youngest child 6−11	0.172	2.85	−0.857	7.69
Youngest child 12−16	0.205	3.70	−0.887	4.16
μ	0.950			
n	4,434			
Log-likelihood	−3653.52			

Note: The MRC estimators have been weighted; *n* is unweighted.

Columns 2 and 4 of table 4.1 present the coefficients for MRC and NCDS respectively. These coefficients are statistically different across the two cohorts. Ceteris paribus, the NCDS women have a significantly higher probability of participating and participating full-time (i.e., they display a higher intercept than those in the earlier cohort), but this probability is not just due to their higher human capital characteristics, which have reduced positive coefficients. They also show that marriage without children is much less of a disincentive to paid work for the later cohort, and that the deterrent effect of children has less of an age pattern than in 1978.[6] The effect of being an owner-occupier is also much reduced, perhaps as the result of the spread of owner occupation and developments in the housing market.

Table 4.2
Earnings equations for women working part-time, both cohorts pooled

	Parameters	t-values	Means
Constant	−0.486	6.71	
NCDS dummy	1.168	2.72	0.76
Ability at 11	0.003	0.00	47.58
O-levels	0.096	0.20	0.37
A-levels	0.213	0.84	0.07
Diploma	0.665	2.07	0.12
Degree	0.759	3.31	0.06
Work experience, 18–25	0.010	0.00	5.25
Work experience, 26–32	0.059	0.02	1.29
Work experience dummy	−0.017	0.01	4.91
Service	0.010	0.00	3.33
Southeast	0.099	0.25	0.21
λ	0.112	0.21	0.08
Log wage			1.08
Adj R^2	0.84		
n	1,119		
F	422.57		
DF	12,972		

Note: The MRC estimators have been weighted; n is unweighted.

Earnings Equations

Once we had an estimate of heterogeneity in labor-force attachment from the participation analysis, we proceeded to test whether the earnings equations are the same for the MRC and NCDS cohorts. These tests detected intercohort differences for both men and women working full-time, but not for part-timers (see Makepeace et al. 1997). For the part-timers, we therefore pooled the sample, and estimated an extended version of equation (4.2) that includes an NCDS intercept to allow for inflation between 1978 and 1991. This is shown in table 4.2. As expected, the earnings of women working part-time increase with education, recent job experience, job tenure, and with being located in the Southeast. The selection term is positive and significant, suggesting the existence of some (positive) selection bias in the part-time labor market.

Our tests among full-timers show that men and women enjoy significantly different rewards to their human capital characteristics. We therefore present separate equations for the two groups of workers. Table 4.3

Table 4.3
Earnings equations for women working full-time

	MRC			NCDS		
	Parameters	t-values	Means	Parameters	t-values	Means
Constant	−0.278	1.16		0.712	6.74	
Ability at 11	0.000	0.09	53.35	0.005	7.22	48.88
O-levels	0.272	4.83	0.30	0.048	0.19	0.33
A-levels	0.544	3.63	0.13	0.253	3.32	0.10
Diploma	0.575	3.11	0.08	0.447	5.95	0.19
Degree	0.907	6.79	0.07	0.593	9.93	0.17
Work experience, 18–25	0.010	0.85	5.73	0.015	2.28	6.14
Work experience, 26–32/33	0.046	1.56	1.31	0.067	6.20	2.48
Work experience dummy	−0.007	0.29	4.82	−0.020	1.95	7.31
Service	0.009	1.14	4.05	0.010	5.84	7.54
Southeast	0.058	1.06	0.29	0.115	4.60	0.21
λ	0.054	0.92	1.02	−0.033	0.80	0.61
Log wage			0.43			1.80
Adj R^2	0.34			0.37		
n	263			1,421		
F	13.21			76.34		

Note: The MRC estimators have been weighted; n is unweighted.

presents the estimation of the earnings equations for women working full-time. In 1978, the education variables appear as the major determinants of earnings. By 1991, job experience and tenure had become important and the rewards to education, by now less unusual, appear to have declined for this group of workers. This contrasts with the much-publicized increase in the rewards to education experienced by male workers over the 1980s (Schmitt 1995 and Gosling et al. 1994). However, they are in line with findings by Harkness (1996), who takes data for women of all ages from the General Household Survey (GHS) and the British Household Panel Study (BHPS) to cover the period 1973–93.

The coefficients of the women's selection terms are insignificant for women full-timers in both cohorts. This result may surprise a convinced believer in unobserved sources of selection. However, it accords with earlier analysis by Joshi and Newell (1989) for the MRC cohort and adds to the lively debate on the extent, direction, source, and measurability of selection bias in earnings equations, summarized for example in Neumark and Korenman 1994. There are many reasons why we may fail fully to

Table 4.4
Earnings equations for men

	MRC			NCDS		
	Parameters	t-values	Means	Parameters	t-values	Means
Constant	−0.393	1.38		0.694	8.02	
Ability at 11	0.007	5.52	50.58	0.004	8.86	45.44
O-levels	0.102	0.03	0.15	0.115	6.22	0.25
A-levels	0.212	0.98	0.13	0.283	3.23	0.20
Diploma	0.259	1.20	0.13	0.426	4.88	0.16
Degree	0.525	2.57	0.11	0.592	7.39	0.15
Work experience, 18–25	−0.002	0.08	7.19	0.015	1.47	6.93
Work experience, 26–32/33	0.107	0.34	2.30	0.094	8.57	3.22
Work experience dummy	−0.007	0.25	5.80	−0.014	1.27	7.64
Service	−0.008	3.27	4.73	0.003	2.61	7.98
Southeast	0.126	5.33	0.29	0.180	10.67	0.20
Log wage			0.73			1.97
Adj R^2	0.30			0.28		
n	1,051			3,098		
F	45.97			121.44		

Note: The MRC estimators have been weighted; n is unweighted.

pick up an existing selection bias, but our result may also be due to our ability to observe in the cohort studies some of the heterogeneity not usually measurable in cross-sectional sources, such as ability. Another possible reason for not detecting unobserved heterogeneity is that the cohort samples have abstracted from variation associated with looking across a range of ages.

Finally we note two rather surprising things about the results for the males as reported in table 4.4. The first is that work experience does not appear to affect wages in the MRC, while it has a positive and, if recent, strong effect on men's wages in NCDS. The second is that the time spent with the same employer appears to reduce wages in the 1946 cohort but increase them in NCDS. The MRC finding for job tenure, unusual as it may be, is consistent with earlier finding by Joshi and Newell (1989) and suggests that these youngish men were benefiting from changing jobs. The changed role of job tenure in 1991 may reflect the increased importance of implicit contracts and internal labor markets over the 1980s. For NCDS a year of recent work experience raised men's wages by 9.9% or 10.2% if it was continuous service with the current employer.

Overall this human capital specification of the earnings equation explains around 30% of the variation in pay among full-timers for both MRC and NCDS (30% and 28% respectively for men and 34% and 37% for women full-timers). The joint specification for part-timers on the two cohorts explains around 84% of the variation of earnings among women part-time employees.

Decomposition of Wage Gaps for Average Workers

We now consider comparisons across the three tables for the three groups of earners. Since they enjoy statistically different remuneration to human capital, it is appropriate to use the Oaxaca-Blinder decomposition of the gross gender gap, as presented in chapter 2. This breaks down the log wage gap into a portion explained by differentials in attributes and one that summarizes the difference in parameters. The former puts a value on any net difference in productive attributes between men and women. The latter is conventionally used as an indicator of discrimination in the remuneration of given attributes. In measuring the extent of labor-market discrimination experienced by women, it is conventional to weight parameter differences by the characteristics of the average woman. This entails a corresponding weighting of attribute differences by men's parameters. We generally use this conventional form of weighting, decomposition (a) in table 4.5, taking the average woman employed full-time as the standard for characteristics. This also shows an alternative decomposition (b), weighting parameter differences by the attributes of men and of women employed part time. The results are reported in table 4.5 and figure 4.1.[7]

The Full-time Gender Gap

On this basis, the crude actual gender pay gap among full-timers, expressed as log of wages, was 0.305 in 1978. Of this, around one-third (0.091) was explained by women having, on average, a lower level of human capital than men, while 0.214 was to be attributed to unequal rewards to these characteristics. By 1991, after more than a decade of equal opportunity legislation, the crude gap had dropped considerably, to almost half its former value, 0.167. In 1991 only one-fifteenth of the differential (0.011) was due to differences in the average stock of human capital held by the two sexes. The remaining 0.156 reflected unfavorable treatment of women workers in the full-time labor market.

Table 4.5
Decomposition of differences in log wages

		Full-timers (men/women)		Women (part-timers/full-timers)	
		MRC 1978	NCDS 1991	MRC 1978	NCDS 1991
Crude gap		0.305	0.167	0.335	0.392
Decomposition (a)	gaps in characteristics	0.091	0.011	0.142	0.172
	parameter gap	0.214	0.156	0.193	0.220
		(0.052)	(0.012)	(0.030)	(0.025)
Decomposition (b)	gaps in characteristics	0.074	0.003	0.201	0.271
	parameter gap	0.231	0.164	0.134	0.121
		(0.042)	(0.012)	(0.037)	(0.022)
Discrimination	D_f	23.9	16.9	21.3	24.0
Coefficient (%)	D_m/D_p	26.0	17.8	14.3	12.9

Notes:
Decomposition (a) weights the parameter gap by the characteristics of full-time females.
Decomposition (b) weights the parameter gap by the characteristics of males for the male-female comparison and by the characteristics of women part-timers for the part-time/full-time comparison.
The standard errors of the parameter gap differential are given in parentheses.
D_f is defined as in equation (2.3).
D_m/D_p refer to the "discrimination index" of males and part-timers respectively and are defined as in equation (2.4).

Thus the main reason for the narrowing of the full-time gender gap is women catching up on men in productivity-related characteristics. This means that less pay difference can be attributed to different human capital in 1991 than in 1978. Men's higher level of human capital, notably via experience and education, accounted for 0.091 of their higher mean log wage in 1978 but only 0.011 in 1991. Differences in estimated rewards to human capital continued to be the major component, and changed less, from 0.214 to 0.156. Given the estimated margin of error of these terms (roughly twice the number reported in brackets in table 4.5), the change over time is not statistically significant. Our results are in accordance with analysis on employees of all ages by Blackaby et al. (1997) who, using the GHS for 1973 to 1991, suggest that, as from 1983, the driving force behind the drop in the crude gender gap is the convergence of the productivity-related characteristics with a modest contribution from the coefficients. Comparing the 1983 GHS with the 1992–93 BHPS, Harkness (1996) reports the narrowing skills gap and improved remuneration

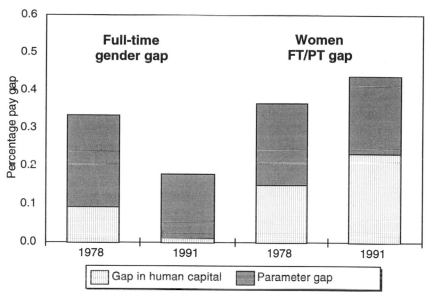

Figure 4.1
Pay gaps in the two cohorts analyzed

accounting for converging rates in roughly equal amounts. Over the previous period she studied, 1974–83, parameter differences changed more, as one would expect given the timing of the Equal Pay Act. Her conclusion that parameter changes predominate over a longer period is thus compatible with our finding that, for a shorter time span and a narrow age band, parameter changes were modest, if any.

With our discrimination coefficient—defined as in (2.3)—dropping by 7 percentage points (from 23.9% to 16.9%), there does appear to have been a reduction in discrimination, but not its elimination. Indeed, the impression of a reduction may be illusory, given the estimated margin of error. The apparent reduction in gender gap may all be due to the closing attribute gap.

The Gap between Women's Wages in Full- and Part-time Jobs

In the analyses of the wages in full-time and part-time sectors of the women's labor market, the overall gap moved in the opposite direction, opening up from 40% of part-timers' pay in 1978 (0.335) to 48% (0.392) in 1991 (decomposition (a) in table 4.5). The increase in the differential was almost equally split between differences in characteristics and differential rewards to those characteristics. Differences in the characteristics increased by 4 percentage points (from 15% to 19%, or from 0.142 to 0.172 in log wages) on average (decomposition (b)). So did the parameter gap (from 21% to 25%, from 0.193 to 0.220 in log wages). Thus weighted, the discrimination coefficients for part-time workers rose over the 1980s from 21% to 26%. Harkness's (1996) analysis of workers of all ages suggests small but increasing unequal treatment of part-timers, opening up by the 1980s to 0.064 in 1992/3.

On the basis of these decompositions, women have made gains in the full-time labor market over the 1980s, both in the accumulation of endowment and in the rate at which it is remunerated. Wages of women working part-time, however, have moved in the opposite direction. This is due to the deterioration in their endowment relative to women working full-time but also to a distinct worsening of their terms of trade. The abolition of the wages councils in the late 1980s, and the fact that there was nothing like the equal pay legislation to force the narrowing of the gap between women in rates of remuneration, may account for the deterioration in the pay condition of part-timers.

Alternative Decompositions

Are these conclusions robust to alternative measures of how to break down the wage gap? In decomposition (b), when the decomposition of the full-time male/female gap is calculated as it affects the average man—that is, weighting parameter differences by male attributes—the results for full-timers change only marginally. Thus weighted, the discrimination rates are 26% in 1978 and 18% in 1991. The parameter gap is therefore marginally larger for both cohorts and so is its change (7 percentage points or 0.067 in log terms), though still not significantly different from zero. With attributes valued at full-time female rates, the gap explained in the first place was smaller, and little further fall was apparent.

The Distribution of Unequal Treatment

Has the treatment of some women improved more than that of others? The major aim of this chapter was to assess how far the experience of unequal treatment has changed from the early years of equal pay implementation to the beginning of the 1990s. We have tackled this issue using the Oaxaca-Blinder decomposition of the average pay gap. This average approach provides a useful summary measure of discrimination, but it neglects differences in the experiences across individual employees. Thus it does not distinguish between one hypothetical labor market where nobody is unequally treated with one where half of the women are paid 5% less than equally productive men, but the other half are paid 5% more. According to equation (2.3) in chapter 2, the discrimination coefficient D_f emerging from both markets would be zero. However, while discrimination is obviously absent from the first market, it is present in the second since unequal treatment exists as long as at least one worker is unequally remunerated. "Equality at the means ... is a necessary but not sufficient condition for the absence of discrimination" (Jenkins 1994).

In response to this observation, some literature has moved beyond the analysis of the average gap to consider the complete distribution of discrimination (Jenkins 1994; Dolton and Makepeace 1985; Blackaby et al. 1997). This approach is obviously relevant to our analysis. We find that, although the crude gender pay gap between full-timers has declined since the late 1970s, gender discrimination in 1991 is on average not statistically different from that experienced in 1978. We are left wondering whether this is because all women full-timers are now as unequally paid as they were in the late 1970s, or whether the implementation of equal pay laws may have benefited some more than others. This section explores this issue.

When the focus is on the individual worker, k, rather than the average, the unexplained component of any existing wage gap can be redefined as

$$UN^k - \sum (\beta_i - \beta_j) \cdot X_j^k \tag{1.3}$$

and the related discrimination coefficients in equation (2.2) can be expressed for each woman as

$$D_f^k = 1 - \exp \sum (\beta_m - \beta_f) \cdot X_f^k \tag{4.4}$$

and

$$D_m^k = 1 - \exp \sum (\beta_m - \beta_f) \cdot X_m^k. \tag{4.5}$$

This chapter makes an intercohort comparison of the distribution of the individual parameter gaps. Employees in the disadvantaged group of women full-timers or part-timers respectively are ranked by the degree of discrimination they are estimated to experience on the basis of their individual X's. An average discrimination index is then computed for each

Table 4.6
Distribution of the pay differential

Percentile	Full-timers (men/women)		Women (full-timers/ part-timers)	
	MRC 1978	NCDS 1991	MRC 1978	NCDS 1991
10	3.0	9.5	6.0	4.9
20	10.6	11.8	11.4	9.9
25	13.1	12.5	13.8	11.8
30	15.9	13.5	16.1	15.3
40	21.5	14.8	22.5	20.6
Median	27.0	16.4	28.3	26.6
60	31.6	18.1	32.4	32.2
70	36.4	20.0	36.6	38.4
75	39.6	21.2	39.3	39.8
80	43.3	22.6	42.1	41.2
90	54.1	25.2	52.6	44.0
100	75.5	37.8	76.1	55.2
Mean	27.8	17.0	28.3	25.5
Standard deviation	20.5	6.2	17.7	15.5
Coef. of variation	0.7	0.4	0.6	0.6
Interquartile ratio	1.0	0.5	0.9	1.1

Note: The MRC estimators have been weighted; n is unweighted.

decile of D_f. The resulting distribution of this index among full-timers in the two cohorts is presented in the first two columns of table 4.6. The next two columns report the distribution of the discrimination index for women part-timers.

In these models, where different attributes receive varying degrees of unequal treatment, each person's experience depends upon individual characteristics. Some endowments receive better remuneration when held by women, where $\beta_m - \beta_f < 0$. In the MRC this applies to the educational attainments, but the unequal remuneration of ability and experience favors men. Among the MRC women, those facing the most discrimination would be those with uninterrupted work experience and high ability who did not have educational qualifications. Conversely, women suffering least unequal treatment would be highly qualified but with low experience and ability. Such cases may be unusual, but it is not immediately obvious whether they would be drawn from the extremes of the wage distribution.[8]

In the NCDS regressions, the women who would be most discriminated against would have O-level qualifications and high experience with employers other than the present one. Formal qualifications in this cohort protect women against unequal treatment only if they have education beyond A-levels, and even then, the protective effect is smaller. Cases with particularly low estimated gender penalties would combine a diploma, continuous employment with the same firm, and high ability. Women with no qualifications and little experience also appear relatively well treated. The association of the gender penalty with the individual wage is not systematic. Those who suffer most discrimination in 1991 are not necessarily the worse paid.

The 20% of the MRC women full-timers who face least discrimination have a lower discrimination coefficient than their NCDS counterparts. All the others, however, face a higher gender premium than the 1958 cohort, with peaks of 54.1% for the least well treated 10%. This suggests a reduction in the spread of the distribution, which is confirmed by the drop in the standard deviation from 20.5 to 6.2. Equal pay appears to have improved the treatment of the majority of women working full-time, especially those very highly discriminated against, but to have increased discrimination for the 20% who had been relatively best treated. The aggregate result is a statistically insignificant change in the extent of discrimination suffered by the average woman full-timer in the two cohorts.

The situation of part-timers appears rather different. On the whole, the "discrimination" index for the 1958 cohort is lower than for the earlier one. It is only the unlucky part-timers in the seventh and eighth decile who suffer worse remuneration in 1991 than those in a similar position did in 1978. The 1980s therefore have seen a shift to the left of the distribution of the discrimination coefficients among part-timers, but the spread has been hardly affected (i.e., the standard deviation has declined only marginally from 17.7 to 15.5).

In a related paper (Makepeace et al. 1997) we explore the distribution of discrimination and locate it in the earnings distribution. More sophisticated techniques allow us to attach a different value to discrimination at different points, that is, different "degrees of discrimination aversion" (Jenkins 1994). Jenkins's summary measure shows discrimination among full-timers and between women working full-time and part-time to be declining over the 1980s for all acceptable values of the degree of discrimination aversion. Only when discrimination against the worse-off women is given a very high weight—that is, the discrimination aversion term exceeds 30—does gender discrimination among full-timers appear to be worse in 1991 than in 1978.

We also conclude that gender discrimination in full-time work is higher among the better paid and that this phenomenon is more pronounced in 1991 than in 1978. Again thesefindings are in accordance with those by Harkness (1996) and Blackaby et al. (1997), which compare respectively crude gender earnings ratios and the adjusted gender gap by percentile of earnings. Women in "top" jobs do seem to have benefited from equal opportunities.

Conclusion

The disadvantages of being female in the full-time British labor market probably did weigh less heavily in the 1990s than they did at the end of the 1970s, although our evidence is not strong enough to exclude the possibility of no change. This conclusion applies to people in their early 30s in full-time employment. We have some reason to believe that other age groups had a similar experience. Indeed, as noted in chapter 1, the published series for the relatively homogeneous group of full-time workers in manual occupations shows little change in the gender ratio over this period.

Equal pay legislation appears to have sustained the position of women in the full-time labor market. Their relative disadvantage, however, has by no means been eliminated: the measured characteristics of the average female full-timers would attract a 17% premium if held by a man. Moreover, while the treatment of women working full-time at most parts of the discrimination distribution has improved, in the least discriminated quartile it worsened.

In 1991, the disadvantages of being a woman are compounded if she is constrained to take a part-time job. Although the low pay of part-timers is partially explained by the fact that average qualifications in this sector are lower than in the full-time labor market, they appear to be penalized even relatively to women with comparable attributes in full-time employment. This penalty has declined only marginally over the 1980s, but the improvement appears to be evenly spread.

Although the slow progress of equal opportunity policies in closing the full-time wage gap can be applauded with at least two cheers, the very slow progress in the part-time sector continues to cause concern both about fairness and about the efficiency of resource allocation. In the next chapter we bring in information about the markets in which the services of human capital are offered, and in the following one we consider further the labor-market constraints imposed on women by the home. These should tell us more about how, why, and for whom unequal pay persists.

5 Do Job Characteristics Explain Unequal Pay?

This chapter introduces features of the job as factors to explain pay differentials in addition to personal characteristics. This adjusts wages for differentials generated, for a number of possible reasons, by the varying nature of employment. Any remaining pay difference between groups of workers represents unequal treatment within type of job. The models, for NCDS data only, introduce information on human capital, firm characteristics, the nature of the job contract, and occupation. They account for less of the full-time gender gap than the gap between women's rates in full- and part-time jobs.

This chapter brings job characteristics into the account of the pay gaps experienced by the young British adults in the 1958 cohort in 1991. It looks beyond the different human capital characteristics of male and female workers to differences in the employers they work for, to the jobs they do and the labor markets in which they operate, and to unequal treatment within each part of the labor market. Because there was less information on jobs in the MRC survey, this analysis is performed on NCDS data only. This means that in contrast to chapter 4, our choice of human capital variables is not limited by what is available to us from the 1946 study.

The main aim of this chapter is to explore how far conditions in the labor market explain variations in men's and women's hourly pay not accounted for by differences in human capital characteristics. Wage differentials adjusted for such characteristics are often used to measure discrimination. However, as suggested in chapter 2, wage differences between equally productive workers may arise from various labor-market conditions. Some of these can be thought of as mechanisms through which discrimination operates, while others lead to unequal outcomes without discrimination being the motive. We use evidence on the type of firm, the characteristics of the particular contract, proxies for the degree of bargaining power, and the occupations of 33-year-old workers to investigate these possible mechanisms.

One sort of job characteristic pervades the analysis: whether or not a woman's job is part-time. This factor is a major correlate of low pay, affecting the relationship of women's pay to other variables as well. Our analyses, therefore, also allow for interactions between women's personal and job characteristics and part-time employment. Another aim of this chapter is to ask whether job characteristics help account for the gap between part-time and full-time rates for women as well as the gap between women and men full-timers, and thereby the gap between men (full-time) and women part-timers.[1]

In the explanation of wage variations, job characteristics modify the estimated direct effects of human capital, but they do not rob them of independent explanatory power. Our estimates suggest that job characteristics supplement human capital variables rather than replace them. We find that the combined effect of systematic gender differences in all these variables (job and personal characteristics) accounts for about half of the 40% wage gap between men and all women (expressed as a percent of the average woman's pay across full-time and part-time jobs). The remaining part (15% of women's pay) is an upper-bound measure of unequal treatment within type of job.

Data and Variable Definition

The data used in this chapter come exclusively from the National Child Development Study (NCDS) of a cohort born in 1958. Their definitions are set out in appendix 3.1. As in the previous chapter, we estimate separate earnings functions for men (full-time) and women, employed full-time and part-time. As so few men worked part-time, the only part-time jobs considered are women's. The dependent variable is again the log of the gross hourly wage earned in a typical week. The sample selected has slightly higher wages on average among full-timers and marginally lower wages for the somewhat depleted sample of part-timers.[2] Both wage differentials are marginally higher than for the samples used in chapter 4. Employment experience has been redefined since chapter 4 as that between the two most recent sweeps of NCDS (23 to 33).[3] In addition to the educational variables used in the previous chapter, the simplest human capital earnings function (model 5.1) includes a dummy reflecting whether any training course longer than three days had been undertaken. After this new human capital model (model 5.1), the second specification, model 5.2, includes additional variables reflecting the characteristics of the employer:

• the size of the firm, with indicators for small firms (<25 employees) and large ones (>100);

• private sector as opposed to a public or nonprofit enterprise;

• industry (based on the 1992 Standard Industrial Code);

• whether the individual lives in London or the Southeast and is presumably employed there.

These variables are included to reflect the extent of monopoly power and the institutional factors on the demand side of the labor market (see, for example, Green et al. 1996). However, the firm size may also be taken as a proxy for the extent to which the employer operates some form of internal market, as this is more common in larger firms, where full information on individual productivity is more difficult to achieve. Thus the sign of the "large firm" dummy is expected to be positive and that of the "small firm," negative. Controlling for private ownership of the firm allows for the higher degree of flexibility in the pay structure of this sector. The industry terms distinguish more buoyant (e.g., service) from declining (e.g., manufacturing) sectors of the economy. The omitted category is "other manufacturing" and any other with a coefficient not significantly different from zero. The regional term reflects some form of compensating differential for working in the expensive Southeast. It is arguably a characteristic of the employee as well as the firm, and is treated as such in chapters 4 and 6.

Model 5.3 controls for characteristics of the individual's particular contract of employment by including additional variables such as:

• receipt of fringe benefits represented by three most common types;

• flexibility of working time;

• whether the individual supervises other workers;

• time spent traveling to work each day (in minutes);

• membership in a union;

• whether the employer had ever provided or financed training.

The first three variables are intended to indicate the degree of desirability of the job and to pick up compensating differentials. The fringe benefits we count include the availability of a company car/van for own use, the provision of private medical insurance, and membership in an employer pension scheme. The time spent traveling to work is intended as a proxy for the degree of monopsony power of the employer along the lines discussed in chapter 2 and, more extensively in Manning (1996), though it may also itself be determined by the rate of pay. Union membership is intended to reflect the other side of the coin: the workers' degree of bargaining power on the supply side. The provision of training by the current employer, likely to be firm specific though not necessarily so, is seen as a proxy for the presence of some form of internal market (Felstead 1995).

Finally model 5.4 introduces two types of information on occupation. First we add a roughly hierarchical banding of occupations reflecting rungs on a career ladder, and possible "glass ceilings." Second we characterize occupations in terms of whether they are likely to be done mainly be women. On its own this would isolate occupations that were segregated by sex. Allowing also for vertical segregation makes this term an indicator of horizontal separation of men's and women's jobs within tiers of the vertical hierarchy. On the vertical dimension, occupations—defined in terms of the three-digit Standard Occupational Classification (SOC)— were grouped into eight bands, virtually the finest classification computationally feasible to incorporate in our models. Semi- and unskilled jobs are the reference category, unskilled jobs being too small in number to treat separately.[4] The idea is to see whether vertical sex segregation between the banded occupations and horizontal segregation between "feminized" and "masculine" jobs are mechanisms making equal pay legislation less than perfectly effective. Even with the equal pay for equal value ("comparable worth") amendment to the Equal Pay Act, it is more difficult to claim equal pay when male comparators are hard to find.

Hakim (1996) suggests that vertical obstacles are more important than horizontal segregation in denying high pay to women. She cites Sloane (1990), who found that three-quarters of the gender pay gap in the New Earnings Survey Panel was accounted for by vertical differences within occupation and only one-quarter to differences between occupations. Women's low pay in this view is due to their failure to advance up the occupational ladder rather than a failure to enter the right occupation.

The horizontal segregation of the NCDS member's occupation has been imputed by reference to the British all-age sex ratio of employees in each of the OPCS 1990 occupational unit groups, taken from the 1991 Census. This is a very fine classification, distinguishing some 370 different types of job. Occupations that had more than 50% females in the national data were classified as "feminized," and cohort members were given a positive value on this dummy if they were reported in such an occupation.[5] It is worth noting that this definition of segregation (of occupation) does not tell us about workplace segregation. There may be more segregation in practice than we can pick up from occupational data.

Results

Hourly wages at the geometric mean were £7.38 for men, £6.14 for women employed full-time, and £4.04 for women part-timers. The men's wages were 20% higher than the full-time women's and 83% ahead of the part-timers, while the differentials between women working full-time and part-timers was 52%. Our results are summarized in both percentages and logarithms in table 5.5. The log of the ratio for men to full-time women was 0.183, full-time women to part-time women 0.419, and men to part-time women 0.602. At the outset there is more of a gap to explain concerning women's part-time employment.

How Much of the Gender Wage Gap Is Explained by Personal Characteristics?

We start by analyzing wage differentials in terms of personal characteristics only (table 5.1). These explain 26%, 36%, and 45% of the variance within each subsample. Coefficients have the expected signs. Education, experience, and having undertaken training all have a strong positive effect on pay in the three markets. We tested whether men, women full-timers, and women part-timers might share the same parameters: they did not.[6] A closer look at the coefficients, indeed, reveals some parameters to be more favorable for part-timers than for women full-timers (for example, the minority of cases with higher education). Likewise the parameters for men are not unambiguously more favorable than for women full-timers.

On balance, differences in "human capital endowment" account for very little of the full-time gender gap. This is 0.183 in logs. Its human capital component is less than one-tenth, 0.017. It is generated mainly by such terms as a one-year lead in work experience, and a six-point lead in the percentage having been trained. This leaves a log gap of 0.166 due to differential rewards to these characteristics (equivalent to 18% of female pay).

Human capital differences are much more evident when we compare women in full-time and part-time jobs: part-timers have 4.3 years less employment experience, a 26% shortfall in training, and lower educational

Table 5.1
Log wages analyzed by personal attributes, NCDS 1991

Variable	Men full-timers			Women full-timers			Women part-timers		
	Parameters	t-value	Means	Parameters	t-value	Means	Parameters	t-value	Means
Constant	1.253	26.92		1.121	23.77		1.022	24.97	
Ability at 11	0.004	6.32	45.59	0.005	5.98	49.64	0.001	1.35	45.45
O-level	0.120	4.84	0.24	0.060	1.95	0.34	0.091	3.08	0.39
A-level	0.149	5.44	0.19	0.091	1.83	0.08	0.123	1.49	0.05
Diploma	0.286	10.05	0.17	0.296	8.45	0.18	0.477	9.18	0.12
Degree	0.472	15.50	0.16	0.415	10.07	0.18	0.692	7.69	0.07
Training	0.121	6.69	0.56	0.174	7.47	0.50	0.172	4.96	0.24
Work experience, 23–33	0.030	7.60	10.06	0.014	3.44	9.09	0.015	3.27	5.81
Service	0.002	1.21	7.98	0.009	4.53	7.13	0.012	3.10	3.55
Log wage			2.00			1.82			1.40
Adj R^2	0.261			0.363			0.447		
n	1,797			866			504		
F	80.133			62.714			51.904		
	Men/FT women difference			FT/PT women difference			Men/PT women difference		
Raw differential, of which:	0.183			0.419			0.602		
Parameter gap[a]	0.166			0.211			0.377		
Gap in characteristics	0.017			0.208			0.225		

Notes: a. Parameter differences weighted by means of women full-timers.
Sample with complete information on firm and job characteristics.

attainments. Thus it is not surprising to find 0.208 of the 0.419 gap (52% of part-time pay) explained by such factors, but this still leaves over half of the differentials unaccounted for. The parameter gap between full-timers and part-timers is thus larger than the crude gender gap. Most of this stems from the constant term reflecting the "part-time job effect," the generalized lower rewards to part-time work. Adjusting for personal characteristics reduces the total gap between the pay of men and that of women in part-time jobs from 0.602 to 0.377, or from 83% to 46% of part-timers' pay. In the case of full-timers we are left with 0.166 or 18% of women's pay to investigate.

Are These Differences Explained by the Women Being in Different Sorts of Firms?

The next step is to include information about the firm (table 5.2). While there is little gender and part-time/full-time difference in the proportion of the sample interviewed in the Southeast, the mean values of the other additional variables vary considerably across groups. The inclusion of this information therefore increased the variation explained in each sample noticeably (by 7 to 11 percentage points).

Part-timers are much more likely than the others to work in small firms and less likely to be in the largest. Men are most likely to be in the private sector and female full-timers the least. The most striking differences between subgroups, however, are in the industrial sector in which they work. The highest concentration of men is in Machinery and Equipment, Transport, and Business Services (13%, 11%, and 10% respectively). The major employer of women working full-time is the Finance sector (11%), followed by Business Services and Education (each 8%). Part-timers, on the other hand, are most numerous in Catering (10%), with Finance and Education each employing only 7% of this group.

After inspecting separate models for women in full- and part-time employment, we pooled the female sample,[7] allowing for differences in the coefficients of only some variables by including their interaction with a dummy for part-time employment. The $\bar{R}^2$ of the pooled regression was 0.57. Separate effects only need be specified for the intercept and three other variables. The introduction of firm-specific variables helped account for the full-time/part-time pay gap insofar as the part-time workers appear to concentrate in low-paying types of firm. For example, employment in either a small firm or the private sector reduces any woman's wage. The fact that more part-timers are in small firms helps account for their low

Table 5.2
Models of log wages analyzed by personal and employer characteristics

Variable	Men full-timers Parameters	Men full-timers t-value	Women full-timers Parameters	Women full-timers t-value	Women part-timers Parameters	Women part-timers t-value	All women Parameters	All women If part time	All women t-value	If part time t-value	Mean of X Men FT	Mean of X Women FT	Mean of X Women PT
Constant	1.326	26.73	1.163	21.70	1.168	23.70	1.163		22.40				
Personal													
Ability at 11	0.003	5.47	0.004	5.17	0.000	0.47	0.004	−0.004	5.23	2.94	45.59	49.64	45.45
O-levels	0.112	4.71	0.064	2.25	0.060	2.22	0.064		2.24		0.24	0.34	0.39
A-Levels	0.114	4.55	0.098	2.26	0.096	1.39	0.098		2.26		0.19	0.08	0.05
Diploma	0.250	9.46	0.309	8.53	0.443	8.19	0.309	0.134	8.69	2.21	0.17	0.18	0.12
Degree	0.423	14.25	0.410	9.47	0.625	6.91	0.410	0.215	10.33	2.86	0.16	0.18	0.07
Training	0.088	5.13	0.142	6.43	0.134	3.88	0.142		6.52		0.56	0.50	0.24
Work experience, 23–33	0.024	6.43	0.012	3.01	0.011	2.72	0.012		3.53		10.06	9.09	5.81
Service	−0.000	0.09	0.006	3.04	0.010	3.09	0.006		3.00		7.98	7.13	3.55
Employer													
Small firm	−0.108	4.09	−0.078	2.70	−0.048	1.44	−0.078		2.75		0.21	0.27	0.47
Large firm	0.067	3.43	0.047	1.87	0.036	1.12	0.047		1.85		0.54	0.47	0.32
Private sector	0.014	0.79	−0.015	0.56	−0.110	4.13	−0.015	−0.095	0.60	2.45	0.67	0.53	0.58
Industry													
Business services	0.127	3.75	0.154	3.53	0.113	1.64	0.154		3.88		0.10	0.08	0.06
Catering	−0.331	2.89	−0.317	3.33	−0.186	4.37	−0.317		4.91		0.01	0.03	0.10
Miscellaneous services	−0.168	3.64	−0.005	0.06	−0.047	0.94	−0.005		0.09		0.02	0.04	0.06
Education	−0.138	3.34	0.042	0.93	0.036	0.62	0.042		0.99		0.03	0.08	0.07

									Men/FT difference	FT/PT women difference[b]	Men/PT difference
Finance	0.320	7.34	0.205	5.71	0.184	4.35	0.205	5.65	0.06	0.11	0.07
Publishing	0.173	3.28	0.157	2.38	0.027	0.16	0.157	2.13	0.03	0.02	0.01
Textile and leather	-0.111	1.39	-0.120	1.84	-0.224	2.84	-0.120	1.59	0.01	0.02	0.01
Transport	-0.045	1.79	0.073	1.86	0.177	3.11	0.073	1.60	0.11	0.06	0.03
Machinery and equipment	-0.193	0.83	-0.074	1.29	-0.150	3.14	-0.074	1.27	0.13	0.03	0.00
Southeast	0.173	8.30	0.098	3.82	0.133	4.14	0.098	4.04	0.22	0.24	0.17
Log wage									2.00	1.82	1.40
Adj R^2	0.372		0.435		0.525		0.572				
n	1,797		565		504		1,370				
F	51.69		32.70		27.51		43.52				
	Men/FT difference		FT/PT women difference[b]		Men/PT difference						
Raw differential, of which:	0.183		0.419		0.602						
Parameter gap[a]	0.167		0.272		0.339						
Gap in characteristics	0.016		0.247		0.263						

Notes:
a. Parameter differences weighted by means for full-time females.
b. Decomposition of full/part-time wage gap uses parameters from the more parsimonious model.

wages. The parameter gap in full-time and part-time work is now down to 0.172, from 0.211.

Nevertheless there are some gender differences between parameters, such as that for the private sector, which is significantly positive for men and negative—but significant only for part-timers—for women. Possible explanations for this result are the different degree of flexibility of labor contracts in the private and public sector and the greater prevalence of nationally negotiated rates in the latter. Another is that private and public employers have different "tastes" for discrimination.

Could the Gender Wage Gap Be Explained by Differences in Job Type?

Table 5.3 addresses this issue, showing separate equations for all three groups, then two combinations of samples allowing for the group thus pooled. One pools both the men and women in full-time jobs and shows nine different terms, including the constant where women receive different treatment. Similarly, the model pooled across all women shows eight terms for variables where part-timers are significantly differently renumerated, not necessarily for the worse, and not including the constant. The means of the job-specific variables (reported in table 5.4) show that substantial numbers of full-timers, male or female, reported access to some form of fringe benefits (car, pension, or medical insurance), but only a few part-timers do. Some degree of choice over hours was reported by around one-third of both sets of full-timers and 27% of part-timer women. Supervision was most common among men and least among women part-timers, though as many as 26% of these reported supervising others. Travel-to-work time is similar for both sets of full-timers (twenty-seven minutes, on average, for men and twenty-five for women), whereas the part-timers average barely more than fifteen minutes. This may reflect part-timers not being able to afford to travel long distances for relatively short hours of work. However, it is also consistent with the view that the monopsonist conditions of local labor markets are a potential cause of the low pay of part-timers (Machin and Manning 1994). This view is reinforced by the fact that union membership is least common among part-timers.

Employers had paid for training about half the full-time employees, but less than one-quarter of the women part-timers. This echoes the findings of Bynner, Morphy, and Parsons (1996), who found that little training has been offered to (or taken by) women in part-time or intermittent employment, who tend to have poor qualifications (and children). Well-qualified childless women fare almost as well as men in getting employer-supplied training. Breugel and Perrons (1995) argue that a vicious circle of low skill and low training forms part of the perpetuation of the "gender order," the differential structure of opportunities and constraints facing men and women.

Contrary to expectations drawing on the notion of compensating differentials, amenities such as fringe benefits and flexible working time were found to be positively remunerated for both men and women. This may indicate the existence of another sort of mechanism such as a segmented labor market where "good jobs" compensate well in terms of working conditions as well as higher pay. Compensation for the degree of responsibility involved in the job, however, works in the expected direction: supervisors, male or female, get paid around 8% better in full-time jobs, though there is no significant effect for part-timers. As expected, time, and presumably distance, traveled are correlated positively with pay. Union membership is expected to confer a positive premium to pay (Booth 1995). However, we only found this among part-timers, not full-timers. This may be accounted for by the coverage of nonmembers by union agreements in full-time jobs. Part-timers not in unions are less likely to enjoy such "free rider" coverage. Another reason why an underlying union premium may remain uncovered among the full-timers is selectivity of union membership, not investigated here (Hildreth 1997).

The inclusion of this set of job characteristics increases further the variance explained for all subgroups, and reduces the number of parameters on which the groups differ. Also, by another small step, the extent of the wage differential explained by human capital characteristics is increased. The extent of differential rewards to these characteristics, however, is still substantial: 0.143 between male and female full-timers (15%) and 0.097 between full- and part-time female employees (10%), or 0.240 (27%) between full-time men and part-time women.

How Far Do Gender Differences in Occupations Account for Wage Differentials?

Table 5.4 presents the result of including occupation in the earnings equation. We use both a hierarchical banding of occupations and a segregation factor, based on a far more detailed classification. The three sets of employees are unevenly distributed over these occupational categories. Male cohort members tend to be overrepresented in other intermediate and skilled occupations; women full-timers are relatively most common among clerical and other intermediate nonmanual occupations; part-timers

Table 5.3
Models of log wages in characteristics analyzed by personal, employer, and job characteristics

Variable	Split samples					
	Men full-timers		Women full-timers		Women part-timers	
	Parameters	t-value	Parameters	t-value	Parameters	t-value
Constant	1.287	24.7	1.071	20.6	1.077	18.2
Personal						
Ability at 11	0.002	3.6	0.004	5.3	0.001	0.6
O-levels	0.086	3.8	0.030	1.2	0.064	2.4
A-Levels	0.088	3.7	0.040	1.0	0.072	1.1
Diploma	0.188	7.3	0.266	7.7	0.442	7.6
Degree	0.337	11.2	0.331	7.7	0.573	6.6
Training	−0.078	1.9	0.111	1.5	0.228	4.0
Work experience, 23–33	0.019	5.4	0.009	2.4	0.010	2.6
Service	−0.001	0.4	0.005	2.7	0.006	1.8
Employer						
Small firm	−0.109	4.2	−0.067	2.4	−0.030	0.9
Large firm	0.066	3.5	0.026	1.1	0.015	0.5
Private sector	−0.005	0.3	−0.016	0.6	−0.089	3.3
Industry						
Business services	0.091	2.8	0.124	3.2	0.122	1.9
Catering	−0.298	2.9	−0.361	4.1	−0.145	3.5
Miscellaneous services	−0.167	3.8	−0.028	0.4	−0.034	0.7
Education	−0.061	1.4	0.075	1.6	0.074	1.3
Finance	0.256	6.3	0.122	3.5	0.187	4.4
Publishing	0.159	3.2	0.137	2.0	0.026	0.2
Textile and leather	−0.082	1.1	−0.107	1.7	−0.180	2.6
Transport	−0.052	2.1	0.016	0.4	0.134	2.3
Machinery and equipment	0.004	0.2	−0.051	1.0	−0.011	0.2
Southeast	0.142	7.0	0.073	2.9	0.118	3.8
Job						
Training paid by employer	0.141	3.4	−0.014	0.2	−0.132	2.3
Hours flexible	0.060	3.3	−0.002	0.1	0.075	2.6
Supervision	0.082	4.7	0.076	3.7	0.003	0.1
Travel-to-work (minutes)	0.002	4.2	0.003	5.2	0.002	1.1
Union member	−0.003	1.6	−0.029	1.3	0.107	3.5
Fringe benefits						
Company car	0.073	4.1	0.124	4.2	0.060	1.0
Medical insurance	0.056	3.1	0.065	2.5	0.132	0.3
Pension	0.073	3.3	0.107	4.0	0.084	2.6

All full-timers		If women		All women		If part-timers	
Parameters	t-value	Parameters	t-value	Parameters	t-value	Parameters	t-value
1.287	25.8	−0.216	2.8	1.071	20.4		
0.002	3.7	0.002	1.9	0.004	5.1	−0.004	2.8
0.088	3.8			0.030	1.1		
0.088	3.6			0.040	1.0		
0.188	7.2			0.266	7.7	0.175	2.9
0.337	11.2			0.331	8.6	0.242	3.2
−0.078	1.9	0.189	2.2	0.111	1.6		
0.019	5.5	−0.010	2.0	0.009	2.7		
−0.001	0.4	0.006	2.1	0.005	2.6		
−0.109	4.7			−0.067	2.5		
0.066	3.5			0.026	1.1		
−0.005	0.2			−0.016	0.6	−0.074	1.9
0.091	3.3			0.124	3.3		
−0.298	3.9			−0.361	5.8	0.216	2.8
−0.167	3.3			−0.028	0.5		
−0.061	1.3	0.136	2.1	0.075	1.8		
0.256	7.4	−0.133	2.5	0.122	3.4		
0.159	3.2			0.137	2.0		
−0.082	0.9			0.107	1.8		
−0.052	2.0			0.016	0.4		
0.004	0.1			−0.051	0.9		
0.142	7.7	−0.070	2.2	0.073	3.1		
0.141	3.5			−0.014	0.2		
0.060	3.5	−0.062	2.1	−0.002	0.1	0.078	2.1
0.815	4.8			0.076	3.7	−0.073	1.9
0.002	5.4			0.003	5.4		
−0.027	1.5			−0.029	1.3	0.136	3.3
0.073	4.3			0.124	5.0		
0.056	3.1			0.065	2.6		
0.726	3.6			0.107	4.3		

Table 5.3 (continued)

	Split samples					
	Men full-timers		Women full-timers		Women part-timers	
Variable	Parameters	t-value	Parameters	t-value	Parameters	t-value
Adj R^2	0.423		0.502		0.551	
n	1,797		866		504	
F	46.37		31.12		22.32	
	Men/FT difference		FT/PT women difference**		Men/PT difference	
Raw differential, of which:	0.183		0.419		0.602	
Parameter gap[a]	0.143		0.097		0.240	
Gap in characteristics	0.040		0.322		0.362	

Notes:

a. Parameter differences weighted by means for full-time females.

b. Decomposition of full/part-time wage gap used parameters from the more parsimonious model.

Means of dependent and explanatory variables are shown in table 5.4.

least common in the top group and concentrated in the clerical and service/ retail categories. To some extent, less prestigious occupations appear more common among women, particularly part-timers. The feminization of the occupation, not surprisingly, in general "discriminated" well between our samples. Sixteen percent of the men, 71% of the female full-timers, and 90% of the female part-timers were in jobs mainly done by women— reflecting the "female ghetto" of most part-time jobs. Inclusion of occupation terms in the model again adds to the variance explained, raising the three $\bar{R}^2$s on the unpooled samples to 0.44, 0.52, and 0.59 (men full-time, women full-time, and women part-time respectively), orders of fit not often found in micro survey data. Once differences in occupations are accounted for, many differences across subsamples in parameter estimates disappear. The whole sample is pooled and two separate sets of interaction terms are allowed for. These contrast the two sets of women with men. Only some effects on wages differ across groups and require an interaction term. As more rows have been added to these tables, the fewer columns are needed.

The pooled model has an $\bar{R}^2$ of 0.59, indicating that well over half of the variance in log wages is explained. Five out of the seven occupational categories included have coefficients significantly different from zero. But only the interaction for clerical part-timers has significant positive coefficients. This means that the premium for being in a clerical job over

Table 5.3 (continued)

All full-timers		If women		All women		If part-timers	
Parameters	*t*-value	Parameters	*t*-value	Parameters	*t*-value	Parameters	*t*-value
0.468				0.614			
2,663				1,370			
40.65				37.92			

doing a low-skill occupation is only 0.3% for men, 2.8% for women full-timers, and 17.6% for part-timers. The lack of other interactions suggests the extent of differential treatment within occupations, given other job and firm characteristics, to be minimal. The horizontal segregation variable has an insignificant coefficient, but the vertical segregation indicator already included may have accounted for the crowding of women into low-paying categories. This accords with the views of Sloane (1990) and Hakim (1996), but surprised us in view of the powerful wage-lowering effect we detected using a similar variable based on the 1980 Classification of Occupations earlier (Paci et al. 1995). Among the possible explanations is the more detailed occupation banding and the inclusion of industry in the present model. These changes could render information on the degree of "feminization" of the occupation redundant to the explanation of differentials.

Does difference in occupation account for the pay gaps? Comparing tables 5.3 and 5.4 shows that the inclusion of the occupation (and segregation) variables makes the greatest contribution to explaining differentials between full-timers. At 0.069, however, the effect of differences in characteristics remains limited (just over one-third of the 0.183 crude gender gap among full-timers). On the other hand, accounting for occupation makes a relatively small contribution to explaining the wage gap between women full-timers and part-timers, raising the log gap due to differences in characteristics from 0.322 to 0.357 (38% to 43%).

Differences in the occupational structure of employment adds a similar amount to the explanation of both gaps. Neither of them, however, are fully accounted for. Differential rewards within occupation are still

Table 5.4
Full model of log wages including occupation

Variable	All persons		If woman				Means of X		
			If full-timer		If part-timer		Men FT	Women FT	Women PT
	Parameters	t-value	Parameters	t-value	Parameters	t-value			
Constant	1.260	25.09	−0.174	2.01	−0.222	2.20			
Personal									
Ability at 11	0.002	2.93	0.002	1.98			45.59	49.64	45.45
O-levels	0.084	3.86					0.24	0.34	0.39
A-Levels	0.081	3.44					0.19	0.08	0.05
Diploma	0.158	6.11			0.218	3.31	0.17	0.18	0.12
Degree	0.294	9.71					0.16	0.18	0.07
Training	−0.069	1.79	0.169	2.00	0.280	3.35	0.56	0.50	0.24
Work experience, 23–33	0.019	5.64	−0.012	2.36	−0.011	2.12	10.06	9.09	5.81
Service	−0.000	0.30	0.006	2.28			7.98	7.13	3.55
Employer									
Small firm	−0.112	5.06			0.099	2.27	0.21	0.27	0.47
Large firm	0.069	3.75					0.54	0.47	0.32
Private sector	−0.003	0.13			−0.073	1.82	0.67	0.53	0.58
Industry									
Business services	0.099	3.74					0.10	0.08	0.06
Catering	−0.292	3.93			0.194	2.13	0.01	0.03	0.10
Miscellaneous services	−0.167	3.43	0.149	1.98			0.02	0.04	0.06

Education	−0.154	2.75	0.161	2.06	0.164	1.94	0.03	0.08	0.07
Finance	0.265	7.86	−0.136	2.62	−0.165	2.20	0.06	0.11	0.07
Publishing	0.142	2.98					0.03	0.02	0.01
Textile and leather	−0.083	0.96					0.01	0.02	0.01
Transport	−0.044	1.76			0.192	2.09	0.11	0.06	0.03
Machine and equipment	0.001	0.04					0.13	0.03	0.00
Southeast	0.139	7.78	−0.064	2.08			0.22	0.24	0.17
Job									
If employer paid for training	0.124	3.24			−0.251	2.95	0.53	0.48	0.21
Hours flexible	0.049	2.90	−0.059	2.02			0.34	0.34	0.27
Supervision	0.057	3.32					0.63	0.58	0.26
Travel-to-work (minutes)	0.002	5.17					26.60	25.00	15.38
Union member	−0.015	0.86			0.112	2.73	0.41	0.34	0.22
Fringe benefits									
Company car	0.054	3.27	0.069	1.98			0.43	0.24	0.08
Medical insurance	0.046	2.63					0.40	0.29	0.14
Pension	0.066	3.39					0.76	0.70	0.28
Occupation									
Professionals	0.151	3.99	0.152	1.69	0.072	0.35	0.08	0.03	0.01
Teachers	0.294	4.50	−0.069	0.69	0.209	1.65	0.03	0.08	0.04
Nurses	0.170	2.90	−0.036	0.42	−0.024	0.26	0.02	0.12	0.11
Other intermediate	0.164	5.58	−0.069	1.10	0.034	0.38	0.35	0.26	0.06
Clerical	0.003	0.07	0.028	0.41	0.176	2.51	0.05	0.32	0.28
Service and shop	−0.009	0.17	−0.078	0.93	0.028	0.39	0.03	0.06	0.33
Skilled occupations	0.075	3.03	−0.033	0.49	−0.041	0.53	0.31	0.07	0.05
Feminized	−0.038	1.42	−0.031	0.73	−0.019	0.29	0.16	0.71	0.90

Table 5.4 (continued)

Variable	All persons		If woman				Means of X		
			If full-timer		If part-timer		Men FT	Women FT	Women PT
	Parameters	t-value	Parameters	t-value	Parameters	t-value			
Log wage							2.00	1.82	1.40
Adj R^2	0.586								
n	3,167								
F	39.98								
	Men/women difference		Men/women FT difference		Men/Women PT difference				
Raw differential, of which:	0.337		0.183		0.601				
Parameter gap[a]	0.136		0.114		0.176				
Gap in characteristics	0.201		0.069		0.427				

a. Parameter differences weighted by means for women full-timers

important: they account for 0.114 of the lead that men full-timers maintain over women full-timers (12% of women's pay), and 0.062 (6%) of the lower pay of part-timers.

Discussion

The overview in table 5.5 summarizes the steps we have taken and expresses wage differentials—accounted for by differences in the average attributes and by differential rewards to those characteristics—in terms of percentages of the lower-paid group's average.[8] As shown in figure 5.1, which is based on the human capital model of table 5.1, the starting point was an excess of men's pay over women's of around 40%. This is the combination of 20% among full-timers and 83% between men and part-timers. While around a quarter of the gross gender gap can be explained by differences in the human capital characteristics of male and female workers (see last column, top panel of table 5.5), differences in attributes account for less than 10% of the pay gap among full-timers (first column of top panel of table 5.5).

The decompositions achieved by the successive models 5.1 to 5.4 are shown for the male-female gap among full-timers in figure 5.2 and the full-time/part-time gap in figure 5.3. These show that differences in human capital endowment alone (table 5.1) explain about a half of the differences between part-timers and full-timers among women (0.208 out of a total differential in log wages of 0.419 in figure 5.3, first bar), but explain very little of the male/female gap among full-timers (only 0.017 out of 0.183—figure 5.2, first bar) Figure 5.4 compares men with all women. Personal characteristics account for a 10% lead for men, mostly over the women working part-time, but leave about 28% unaccounted for.

Information about the firm and the industry in which the cohort member is employed (as in table 5.2) adds nothing to the explanation of the gender gap among full-timers (compare columns 1 and 2 of figure 5.2) and only 5 percentage points to the explanation of the pay differential between part-time and full-time women (compare columns 1 and 2 of figure 5.3). That is after controlling for the personal characteristics, which are particularly well documented in a cohort study. Although they are clearly important across individuals within each sex, the role played by these variables in explaining group differences in wages if very limited.

The role of job characteristics is more important (columns 3 of figures 5.2 and 5.3). However, the greatest single contribution to explaining the gender wage gap is given by the introduction of occupations (as in the

Table 5.5
Summary of decompositions

Explanatory model	Full-time men-women	Women full-part-time	F-t men P-t women	F-t men All women
Logarithms				
Table 5.1 Personal characteristics				
Gross differential	0.183	0.419	0.602	0.337
Parameter gap	0.166	0.211	0.377	0.244
Gap in characteristics	0.017	0.208	0.225	0.093
Table 5.2 Personal and firm characteristics				
Gross differential	0.183	0.419	0.602	0.337
Parameter gap	0.167	0.172	0.339	0.230
Gap in characteristics	0.016	0.247	0.263	0.107
Table 5.3 Personal, firm, and job characteristics				
Gross differential	0.183	0.419	0.602	0.337
Parameter gap	0.143	0.097	0.240	0.179
Gap in characteristics	0.040	0.322	0.362	0.158
Table 5.4 Personal, firm, and job characteristics, occupation				
Gross differential	0.183	0.419	0.602	0.337
Parameter gap	0.114	0.062	0.176	0.136
Gap in characteristics	0.069	0.357	0.350	0.201
Percentage of lower pay				
Table 5.1 Personal characteristics				
Gross differential	20.1	52.0	82.6	40.1
Parameter gap	18.1	23.5	45.7	27.6
Gap in characteristics	1.7	23.1	25.2	9.8
Table 5.2 Personal and firm characteristics				
Gross differential	20.1	52.0	82.6	40.1
Parameter gap	18.2	18.8	40.4	25.9
Gap in characteristics	1.6	28.0	30.1	11.3
Table 5.3 Personal, firm, and job characteristics				
Gross differential	20.1	52.0	82.6	40.1
Parameter gap	15.4	10.2	27.1	19.6
Gap in characteristics	4.1	38.0	43.6	17.2
Table 5.4 Personal, firm, and job characteristics, occupation				
Gross differential	20.1	52.0	82.6	40.1
Parameter gap	12.0	6.4	19.2	14.6
Gap in characteristics	7.2	42.9	41.9	22.2
	Men FT	Women FT	Women PT	
Sample size	1,797	866	504	

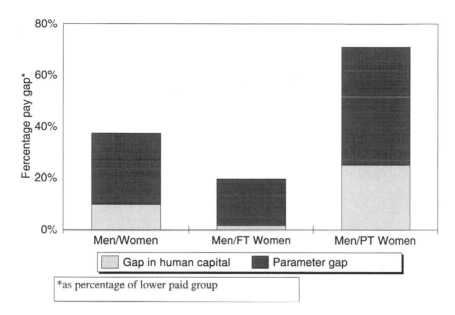

Figure 5.1
Pay gaps in NCDS

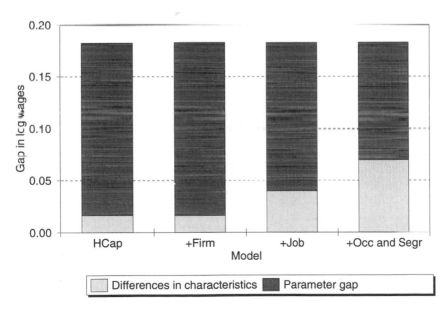

Figure 5.2
Analysis of full-time gender gap

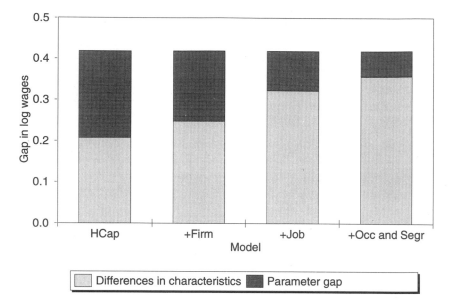

Figure 5.3
Analysis of full- to part-time gap

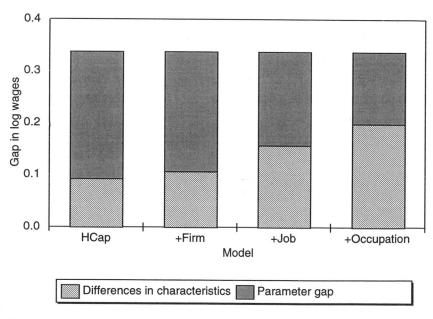

Figure 5.4
Analysis of the overall gender gap

fourth bar of figures 5.2 and 5.3). Figure 5.4 shows that we can explain about three-fifths of the total gap between men and women once gender differences in the occupational distribution are introduced. In table 5.5 a gross gender gap of 40% appears to be the product of about 1.22 and 1.15 from differences in attributes and in parameters respectively. This result is comparable with earlier findings for the United States by Groshen (1991). It also confirms the conclusions by Millward and Woodland (1995) and Harkness (1996) for the United Kingdom. The first British study uses data from the 1990 Workplace Industrial Relations Survey to establish the link between segregation at the firm level and the aggregate gender gap. The second, individual level analysis finds that in 1992–93 at least 85% of the full-time gender gap was left unexplained even after accounting for differences in human capital characteristics, firm size, unionization, region, industry, and occupation.

This exercise has drawn attention to the different rates of pay in full and part-time employment for women. To understand the impact of gender in the labor market, it is necessary to take both segments into account. In the NCDS generation, the full-time employees of both sexes had equivalent education and experience. As Figures 5.1 and 5.2 show, most of the pay gap between them arises out of unequal treatment of equivalent human capital, as far as we can measure it. A comparison of figures 5.2 and 5.3 shows the pay gap between women employed full- and part-time to be larger than the gender gap among full-timers, but also that more of it can be explained at almost all stages. In terms of the personal attributes that might raise their productivity, such as education and experience, part-timers are less well endowed than full timers. They also tend to be found in labor-market situations where their employers may be unable—or unwilling—to pay them at their marginal value product. Such situations may be characterized by monopsony, and would arise if the employer is the only one accessible. As part-timers are relatively less likely to be members of a union, they are also less able to demand high wages. Finally, they are predominantly in low-level, feminized occupations, where wage discrimination would have its greatest impact. The NCDS results agree with the finding of Harkness (1996) that the introduction of "demand-side variables," such as occupation and industry, raises the explained component of the full-time/part-time gap considerably—here from 50% to 85%.

Even after allowing for these factors, the 33-year-old part-timers suffered an otherwise unexplained markdown on their wages of 6%, compounding the gender difference in parameters they would experience even if they were full-timers. Harkness also finds such unequal treatment in some of her models for women of all ages. Lissenburgh (1996) concludes that virtually all of the 32% average difference in the pay of part-timers in the 1992 Employment in Britain Survey was accounted for by characteristics of firms, human capital characteristics, grade, and gender. This means he found no significant within-firm, within-grade, discrimination on pay, but there were disadvantages with respect to fringe benefits, such as pension, sick pay, transport, and private insurance, which we see also here.

The extent of differential treatment we detect is a lower bound of the estimate of sex discrimination in the labor market as a whole, insofar as some of the estimated effects of occupation or firm size may themselves be the mechanism through which discrimination works. The parameter gap in table 5.1 would be nearer such an estimate, provided one accepts that there are no other omitted determinants of excess male productivity and no differences in preference. On the other hand, our failure to account for all of the gaps could be due to inadequate information on the segment of the labor market and insufficient detail on occupation, and it could therefore be viewed as an upper-bound estimate of within-job unequal treatment.

Finally, figure 5.4 shows that gender differences in the distribution of occupations go a long way to explain the pay gap between men and women. Thus some of the unequal treatment is not so much of the gender of workers but of gendered jobs. Vertical segregation appears more effective than horizontal at determining pay. Nevertheless, women in a given occupation are still, all else equal, paid 12% less than men, if full-time, and 19% less if part-time. There still may be a mechanism analogous to the unequal treatment of the sexes whereby the wages of part-timers are marked down. Whether this is part and parcel of the treatment of women, or whether it would apply to male part-timers as well, cannot be disentangled with the evidence available, part-timers being virtually all women.

Conclusion

What has this evidence from the 1958 cohort told us about why men's and women's wages still differ? Combined with evidence on their personal characteristics, the different composition of men's and women's employment accounts for around three-fifths of the wage gap, but it adds surprisingly little to that accounted for by the personal characteristics on their own. We have not been able to find explanations as to why the average 33-year-old woman would have been paid 6% better if she was working in a predominantly male job. While we may have failed to take all relevant factors into account, it could also indicate society's failure to achieve equal treatment in full. Comparison of our findings with those from the previous National Cohort Study is comforting. In 1978 the male to female lead in the pay of 32-year-olds was 58%. The "full model" of Joshi and Newell (1989), which allowed for a somewhat shorter list of firm and job characteristics, explained 24%, leaving 28% due to parameter differences. This is almost twice the gender premium of 15% in the combined NCDS samples. To the extent that parameter gaps reflect unequal treatment, things would seem to have improved over time, though there may still be a way to go.

The availability of fringe benefits seems to magnify rather than compensate inequalities in pay. This is not on the face of it what might be expected from a compensating wage differential. It is, however, consistent with the story of fragmentation of the U.K. labor market into submarkets, some of which offer high pay and good working conditions, while others offer neither of these amenities. Females, especially part-timers, are on the less desirable playing field. An alternative interpretation expounded by Hakim (1996) is that the part-time aspect of the job is in itself an amenity, which allows a lower rate of pay in compensation. If this was the case, it would appear to operate differently from other amenities, which do not appear to reduce wages.

If the travel-to-work term reflects the degree of monopsony prevailing in the market, the evidence is consistent with the predictions of the discriminatory monopsony model, which suggests that wages would be lower for workers with lower elasticity of supply. In this context, the particularly small travel radius of part-timers leads to them having less choice of employer and hence being paid less. The significantly positive coefficient of the term for the minority of part-timers in unions reinforces this interpretation. Unions introduce an element of supply-side monopoly that counteracts the monopsony power of the employer.

Finally, we found that introducing occupation affected the estimated returns to other determinants of earnings. The returns to human capital therefore are partly mediated by sorting into occupations. Coupled with the concentration of women (especially part-timers) in "feminized," low-return occupations, this provides clear evidence of a strong association of occupational segregation and women's low pay.

After allowing for factors on the demand side of the labor market as well as human capital, some differences in the pay of men and women remain. As set out in figure 2.1, these differences may, in part, be due to the higher degree of uncertainty associated with the productivity level of women, especially part-timers (statistical discrimination). The wage gap would then arise from the employers perceiving the productivity level of women to be lower, or less predictable, than that of men. That employers appear to be relatively less prepared to finance training of women (especially part-timers) supports this view. There is also the possibility that "taste-based" discrimination by employers, employees, or indeed, consumers, contributes to wage gaps, particularly between men and women.

Some wage gap remains unexplained after allowing for the sorting of individuals into better- and worse-paying parts of the labor market. This reflects within-job differences in the rewards received by men and women. Unequal pay does not arise wholly out of sorting within the labor market: but some of it does, particularly for women part-timers.

6 Do Family Responsibilities Explain Women's Low Pay?*

This chapter is concerned with the possible impact of family responsibilities, all else equal, on women's rate of pay. We ask whether responsibility for children, in particular, can account for the full-time/part-time pay gap left unexplained in the previous chapters. This question is first addressed by including an indicator of parenthood in the full model of chapter 5 for NCDS. Next we return to the human capital model and to women in both cohorts.

First we isolate the component of the full-/part-time pay gap that is due to family responsibilities. We then do the opposite exercise by indentifying the extent to which the lower pay of mothers is the result of their tendency to work part-time. Finally we introduce a new distinction that can be made for NCDS, between mothers who took maternity leave and then returned to work and those whose employment histories were more disrupted.

The Combination of Childrearing and Paid Work

So far, the analysis of pay differentials has sought explanation in the workers' own productive endowments of human capital and in the labor market circumstances in which the wage is set. This chapter brings in the worker's family responsibilities. Becker (1985) suggests that domestic duties would reduce the effort women were able to put into paid work. The converse suggestion that men with responsibilities as breadwinners would, all else equal, be more motivated and productive is not pursued here. We are interested in family commitments and their effect on women's pay, particularly whether and how they may account for the low pay of part-time jobs. As we consider women in their early 30s, many are at a

---

*Jane Waldfogel is a co-author of this chapter.

stage of life where the demands of young children might reasonably be expected to conflict with paid work.

The chapter returns to the comparison of the NCDS cohort with its predecessor, the MRC National Survey of Health and Development of the 1946 birth cohort. This enables us to see how far any impact of maternal responsibilities on pay may have changed over the 1980s. During the period concerned, labor-market participation of mothers increased, as did awareness of the problems involved in combining employment with child rearing. One relevant contrast between the two cohorts is that the 1946 cohort had mostly entered motherhood before the 1976 Employment Protection Act introduced statutory maternity leave. A far greater proportion of the NCDS cohort would have been able to exercise maternity leave rights, and many did. The analyses of the chapter can also help assess how far this protection of women's employment has helped protect their pay.

Systematic differences have been found within the pay of British women. Groups that have been compared are: (1) full-time and part-time workers (Ermisch and Wright 1992, 1993; Harkness 1996; Makepeace et al. 1997; and chapters 4 and 5 of this book), (2) married women and others (Greenhalgh 1980; Dolton and Makepeace 1987; and Joshi and Newell 1989), and (3) mothers and childless women (Waldfogel 1993, 1995; Joshi and Newell 1989). These results are confirmed by the American literature on the pay penalty to part-time work (e.g., Jones and Long 1979; Corcoran et al. 1983)[1] and on the wage effects of marital status (Hill 1979; Neumark and Korenman 1994) and children (Fuchs 1988; Hill 1979; Korenman and Neumark 1992; Wood et al. 1993; and Waldfogel 1997b). Chapter 4 also shows that the trend is for a growing gap between full-timers and part-timers. The 40% differential found in 1978 between the wages of women employed full- and part-time had risen slightly, to 44%, by 1991.

Theoretically there are various reasons for the existence of a full-time/part-time gap. It may result from a productivity differential between the two groups. However, the analysis of the previous chapters has established that less than half of the full-time/part-time gap can be accounted for by differences in measured human capital endowments. Moreover table 4.5 shows the component of this differential explained by differences in productivity-related characteristics (such as ability, education, and work experience) to have remained relatively unchanged between the 1946 and the 1958 cohorts. The gap may also be associated with characteristics of the job. Chapter 5 shows how, for the 1958 cohort, a considerable part of the full-time/part-time pay gap that is not due to differences in endowments can be accounted for by different types of firm, job, and occupation. However, even after mechanisms such as compensating differentials and low labor-market leverage are taken into account, 6.4% of the part-time penalty remains unaccounted for.

Two possible rationales for this differential have been put forward by the literature. Part-time workers might be less productive than their full-time counterparts or perceived as such by their employers. Alternatively they may have different tastes and different supply elasticities. But why? Family responsibilities are an obvious answer to suggest. In both cohorts, around nine out of ten part-timers had children, twice as many as among full-timers.

Family responsibilities may reduce actual productivity if they limit the level of effort women, faced with a "double burden," are able to put into their jobs, (Becker 1985; Hakim 1996).[2] Moreover, in a labor market with imperfect information, the employer's expectations of the worker's productivity may be negatively affected by her being a mother. This may happen if (1) the employer knows that the productivity of workers with domestic responsibility is on average lower than for others or (2) if there is more variability of their productivity around a common average. In either case, "statistical discrimination" could lead to lower wage offers for workers with family responsibilities. A possible source of such discrimination is the uncertainty surrounding the reliability of child care. For example, unreliable child-care arrangements may genuinely lower productivity (as, for example, mothers may have to spend more time away from work). However, an erroneous presumption by the employer that child care will be unreliable could result in statistical discrimination.

Circumstances at home may also make flexible or reduced working time more attractive. Thus worker preference may lead to a differential compensating for convenience. Family responsibilities also reduce mobility and increase the costs of potential search. This reduces the elasticity of supply and makes workers more vulnerable to monopsonistic behavior of the employer.

Domestic circumstances therefore have a place among the variables that might explain the part-time/full-time pay gap. Any systematic difference between those with and without family commitments may add to the component of the differential explained by other variables. It may also, however, pick up and account for differences hitherto attributed to human capital and job characteristics. One aim of this chapter is to find out how the wage gap between women working full-and part-time can be accounted for by differential family responsibilities. We also look at the "family gap" between the wages of women with and without family responsibilities, to see how far human capital can account for it. In so doing we also allow for just one job characteristic: whether or not the job is part-time.

We take the presence of children in the household as a proxy for family responsibility. Having a partner but not a child appeared to have made little difference to the NCDS participation model (chapter 4). It also adds little to the analysis of wages in the 1946 cohort once the presence of children is controlled for (Joshi and Newell 1989). Partnership was rather crudely defined, following the definition available in MRC, as to whether the cohort member has ever been married (or partnered in NCDS). The MRC study had a small but poorly recorded number who had parted company with their husbands. More (approximately 10%) of the ever-partnered in NCDS reported not having a partner present in 1991. The proportion of women part-timers with partners and with children was high and similar for the two cohorts. In MRC, 97% of the part-timers had ever been married and 89% had children; in NCDS, the figures were 93% and 95% respectively. Of the women working full-time, just under three-quarters, in both cohorts, had ever been married, and just under half had children (45% of MRC and 44% of NCDS full-timers).

We begin the regression analysis of wages by including a dummy variable for being a parent in the full model (including job characteristics and covering men and women) reported in table 5.4. We then move on, using data from both the 1946 (MRC) and 1958 (NCDS) cohorts, to compare the hourly earnings of mothers with those of women with no children. We base these comparisons on a human capital earnings function similar to that used in chapter 4. The use of the human capital model allows us to compare both cohorts. However, it implies that any concentration of mothers in particularly low- (or high-) paid jobs is associated in these estimates with family responsibility, not job type (within full- or part-time segments). It would therefore incorporate both the direct effect of motherhood onto wages—that is, the within-job family gap—and its indirect effect, via differential access to jobs. We do, however, explicitly control for differences in full- and part-time jobs.

Finally, we explore the question of how the length of any interruption of employment around childbearing affects the subsequent fortunes of women in the labor market. We test whether mothers with a minimal gap in employment at their first birth, loosely labeled "maternity leavers," were remunerated differently from either the other mothers or the childless women. This is to see how far access to maternity leave reinforced the effect of equal pay and equal opportunities legislation for women at this stage of life.

The Effects of Family Responsibilities on Participation: A Comparison over Time

Even a superficial comparison of the two cohorts reveals striking differences in the effect of family responsibilities on employment history. The proportion of single women having a job dropped from 90% in 1978 to 74% in 1991. In contrast the equivalent proportions among (ever) married women rose from 40% to 59%, and among all women with children from 17% to 46%. Differentials in participation by family status, though still marked in 1991, had been greater in 1978. The drop among the single can be attributed to unemployment, and, in part, to low rates of employment among single mothers. The percentage of women in part-time employment went up across all family statuses: among the single it was 14% in 1991 compared to 5% in 1978; for married women it went from 30% to 48%; and the proportion of mothers working part-time rose to 55% in 1991 compared to 31% in 1978.

The Method

We begin with the question of whether the higher concentration of mothers in part-time employment contributes to explaining the low average pay this type of work receives. It might be thought that family responsibilities reduce the earning power of mothers in one or more of the ways detailed above. The average low earnings of part-timers, then, would simply reflect the relatively high concentration of low-productivity, low-earning mothers in this type of jobs. To test this hypothesis, in the first instance we simply add a dummy variable for parents to the earnings equations reported in table 5.4. Since the data show that being a parent has a significant negative effect on female wages, we proceed to assess to what extent this pay penalty to motherhood may account for the wage differential between part-timers and full-timers.

We use an innovative decomposition of the pay gap between full- and part-time work. This decomposition isolates three elements of the pay gap: (1) the differential among women without children, (2) a within-mothers component, and (3) a composition effect. The wage differential is therefore decomposed as follows

$$(\bar{w}_f - \bar{w}_p) = (\bar{w}_f^c - \bar{w}_p^c) \cdot g^f + (\bar{w}_f^m - \bar{w}_p^m) \cdot (1 - g^f)$$
$$+ (\bar{w}_p^c - \bar{w}_p^m) \cdot (g^f - g^p), \tag{6.1}$$

where w stands for log wage, the subscripts f and p stand for full-timers and part-timers respectively, the superscripts m and c stand for mothers and childless women, and g^f and g^p are defined as

$$g^f = \frac{C_f}{C_f + M_f} \quad \text{and} \quad g^p = \frac{C_p}{C_p + M_p}, \tag{6.2}$$

with C and M indicating the numbers of childless women and mothers respectively.

In other words, the average log-wage gap between full-time and part-time jobs is a weighted sum of (1) the full-time/part-time differential within childless women, (2) the full-time/part-time differential within mothers;[3] and (3) the product of the family gap within part-timers and the difference in the participation rates of childless women in full-time and part-time employment.[4] The third term is the "composition effect." This measures the extent to which the low pay of part-timers can be explained by the relatively high concentration of mothers in these jobs. This is the magnitude of interest. By comparing the results of this decomposition for the two cohorts, we are able to assess any change in the importance of family responsibilities as a cause of low pay.

To analyze the penalty to part-time work, for each cohort we estimate four separate human capital earnings equations for mothers and childless women in full-time and part-time jobs. A preliminary step was to consider whether sample selection into part-time or full-time employment and the endogeneity of motherhood might bias the wage equation. We begin by estimating, for each cohort, a multinomial logit model that allows for the simultaneous determination of maternal and employment status, distinguishing full-time from part-time jobs. The details of the specification and the estimation are given in appendix 6. A two-step procedure is used to test the status-specific wage equations for selection bias along the lines described in chapter 2 (Heckman 1979; Greene 1992). We allow for the possibility of selection into either motherhood or employment.

Four separate earnings equations are then estimated for each cohort, using information available for both cohorts, including sample selection correction factors. We test for common parameters across equations.[5] The human capital specification resembles that in chapter 4. However, we have now dropped the variable measuring early work experience (18 to 26), which was consistently insignificant throughout. We have included the social class of the woman's father when she was 16. The latter was intended to amplify the rather limited information on the background of the MRC women, of whom a large number had no qualifications (Joshi and Newell 1989). The variables entering the earnings equations are defined in chapter 3.

The standard Oaxaca-Blinder procedure described in chapter 2 is then adopted to further decompose each of the three elements of (6.1). For each motherhood status, $s = c, m$, the decomposition takes the form

$$\overline{w}_F^S - \overline{w}_P^S = \sum (\overline{X}_F^S - \overline{X}_P^S) \cdot \beta_F^S + \sum (\beta_F^S - \beta_P^S) \cdot \overline{X}_P^S, \tag{6.3}$$

where s indicates motherhood status and the bold character indicates a vector of variables. The first term reflects differences in the endowment set X, and the second the impact of different parameters in the vector β. Thus the latter provides a measure of differential remuneration of the endowments of full-time and part-time workers.

In a similar way, we assess the related hypothesis that the relatively low average pay of mothers is due to the relatively high proportion of mothers working part-time. We do so by decomposing the average wage differentials between mothers and childless women according to

$$(\overline{w}^c - \overline{w}^m) = (\overline{w}_f^c - \overline{w}_f^m) \cdot f^c + (\overline{w}_p^c - \overline{w}_p^m) \cdot (1 - f^c)$$
$$+ (\overline{w}_f^m - \overline{w}_p^m) \cdot (f^c - f^m). \tag{6.4}$$

The derivation of and intuition behind this is identical to that of (6.1), where f^c and f^m are defined as

$$f^c = \frac{C_f}{C_f + C_p} \quad \text{and} \quad f^m = \frac{M_f}{M_f + M_p}. \tag{6.5}$$

Once again it is the size of the composition effect, the last component of the sum in (6.4), which provides evidence for the hypothesis tested.

The analysis is finally extended to allow for structural differences between those mothers who have continuous employment history, or minimal gap, at the time of their first child and those who left the labor market around childbearing. We refer to the first group as "maternity leavers," although we do not really know whether each mother with no more than a twelve-month gap was entitled to, or indeed took, statutory maternity leave. We could do this analysis only for the NCDS cohort because a very small number of MRC women had continuous employment around

Table 6.1
Full model of log hourly earnings including parenthood (1958 cohort, men and women)

Variable	Means			Interactions with					
	Men	FT Women	PT Women	Parameters	t-ratio	FT Women	t-ratio	PT Women	t-ratio
Constant				1.122	22.74	-0.010	0.14	-0.194	2.19
Personal									
Ability at 11	45.592	49.137	45.026	0.003	7.41				
O-levels	0.237	0.330	0.384	0.061	4.05	-0.062	2.44		
A-levels	0.194	0.094	0.059	0.094	4.99	-0.079	2.11		
Diploma	0.164	0.191	0.128	0.183	9.47			0.195	3.65
Degree	0.169	0.174	0.060	0.317	14.78				
Training	0.548	0.480	0.229	-0.063	1.70	0.158	2.19	0.268	4.27
Years employed since 23	10.038	9.074	5.889	0.020	4.40	-0.009	1.96	-0.008	1.88
Years in this job	7.937	7.160	3.616	0.003	6.35	0.006	3.00		
Employer									
Southeast	0.193	0.202	0.143	0.154	2.13	-0.078	2.65		
Small firm	0.220	0.253	0.488	-0.086	9.62			0.062	1.86
Large firm	0.529	0.482	0.313	0.067	5.26			-0.056	1.71
Private sector	0.671	0.529	0.574	0.037	5.30	-0.065	2.65	-0.107	3.98
If employer paid for training	0.521	0.458	0.200	0.160	2.71	-0.134	1.87	-0.292	4.51
The job									
Fringe benefit	0.978	0.971	0.914	0.083	2.67				
Hours flexible	0.341	0.336	0.268	0.051	3.63	-0.061	2.42		
Supervision	0.631	0.573	0.259	0.059	5.47				
Travel-to-work (min.)	26.075	24.989	15.508	0.002	5.29	0.002	2.92		
Union member	0.416	0.363	0.223	-0.022	2.00			0.157	5.63

Occupation

Professionals incl. teachers	0.111	0.115	0.045	0.154	5.19	0.108	1.84	0.293	3.28
Intermediate incl.	0.351	0.339	0.169	0.168	6.33	-0.055	1.04	-0.036	0.64
Clerical	0.053	0.290	0.271	0.052	1.31	0.063	1.00	0.138	2.57
Service and shop	0.026	0.058	0.337	-0.005	0.08	-0.043	0.52	-0.010	0.15
Skilled occupations	0.346	0.098	0.069	0.022	1.02	-0.037	0.65	-0.038	0.72
Occupation: Feminized	0.130	0.616	0.904	-0.053	2.08	-0.015	0.41	-0.016	0.29
Parent:	0.625	0.404	0.943	0.054	3.93	-0.096	4.13	-0.069	1.58
Adj R^2				0.55					
n	2,497	1,219	664	4,380					
F				89.97					
Unexplained differential[a]						0.108		0.149	
Explained differential						0.075		0.453	
Total differential						0.183		0.592	

Note. a. Parameter differences weighted by means for full-time females.

childbirth (Macran et al. 1996). An extended version of the multinomial model investigates whether being childless or having taken maternity leave are jointly determined with wages as well as selection into employment status. The details of its specification are given in appendix 6.

What Accounts for the Part-time Pay Gap?

Table 6.1 presents the results of adding a dummy variable identifying parents, men and women, to the full model, human capital plus job characteristics, of table 5.4. The results of this estimation (which only uses NCDS5 data) are as expected and confirm previous evidence. We find that being a parent is associated with higher wages in men, in accordance with findings in the United States (Blackburn 1990; Hill 1979). The association is reversed among women full-timers, as also found in previous research (Waldfogel 1993, 1995). It is perhaps more surprising that parenthood has no significant association with the wage of part-time workers. Harkness (1996), using data on workers of all ages from the GHS and the BHPS, also finds very little extra explanatory information of the part-time/full-time gap when children are introduced. This is an important conclusion for our purposes, since it suggests that it is not the high concentration of mothers in poorly paid part-time jobs that causes the low average pay of part-timers. The story appears to be rather the opposite. Mothers tend to be poorly paid because they tend to take part-time jobs.[6] The rest of this chapter provides a more rigorous justification for this rather controversial statement.

Similar conclusions are drawn from estimating a more parsimonious human capital earnings equation for the women in both the MRC and NCDS cohorts. In our regression samples the average differential in log wages between women working full-time and their part-time counterparts has increased over the 1980s. It was 0.33 in 1977/8 in the MRC and had increased to 0.39 in 1991 for the NCDS. The coefficients of the earnings equations differ for the four subgroups of workers within each cohort: mothers working full-time, childless women working full-time, mothers working part-time, childless women working part-time.[7] The question then becomes where the structural break occurs: within employment status or parental status, or both? We test subsets of samples. The results suggest significant differences by parental status, and by employment status within that. We therefore maintain four separate earnings equations for mothers and childless women in full-time and part-time jobs for both cohorts. The results are presented in tables 6.2 and 6.3.

Table 6.2
Earnings equation for the 1946 cohort in 1977/78ᵃ (employment status within maternal status)

| | Childless women | | | | | | Mothers | | | | | |
| | Full-timers | | | Part-timers | | | Full-timers | | | Part-timers | | |
Variables	Coeffs.	t-ratio	Means	Coeffs.	t-ratio	Means	Coeffs.	t-ratio	Means	Coeffs.	t-ratio	Means
Constant	-0.434	1.20	1.00	-0.851	0.64	1.00	0.369	1.15	1.00	-0.404	2.52	1.00
Education												
Ability at 11	0.008	1.55	51.35	-0.018	2.19	51.71	-0.003	-0.67	52.70	0.003	1.10	50.00
O-levels	0.199	1.95	0.34	0.342	2.56	0.25	0.324	3.35	0.23	0.060	1.15	0.25
A-Levels	0.390	2.90	0.13	0.738	2.97	0.09	0.470	3.56	0.09	0.122	1.47	0.07
Diploma	0.325	2.32	0.10	-0.488	0.98	0.02	0.771	5.63	0.09	0.643	4.43	0.02
Degree	0.673	4.33	0.11	0.600	1.88	0.05	0.718	2.32	0.01	0.719	3.72	0.01
Experience												
Years employed since 23	0.040	0.78	5.44	-0.019	0.48	5.06	0.040	1.99	4.27	0.002	0.18	3.28
Years in this job	0.015	1.74	5.45	-0.017	0.65	3.14	-0.007	0.54	2.69	0.028	2.20	2.16
Others												
Father social class 1 or 2	0.098	0.15	0.21	0.131	0.64	0.15	-0.059	0.52	0.10	0.013	0.19	0.10
Southeast	0.131	0.22	0.32	0.107	0.88	0.22	0.009	0.12	0.23	0.017	0.37	0.21
λ	-0.076	2.19	1.08	0.863	1.72	2.19	-0.197	1.25	1.44	0.224	1.55	0.87
Log wage			0.49			0.15			0.26			0.04
Adj R^2	0.307			0.588			0.322			0.208		
n	150			31			124			279		
F	7.601			5.171			6.835			8.297		

a. The data are weighted.

Table 6.3
Earnings equations for the 1958 cohort in 1991 (employment status within maternal status)

| | Childless women | | | | | | Mothers | | | | | |
| | Full-timers | | | Part-timers | | | Full-timers | | | Part-timers | | |
Variables	Coeffs.	t-ratio	Means	Coeffs.	t-ratio	Means	Coeffs.	t-ratio	Means	Coeffs.	t-ratio	Means
Constant	0.493	2.92	1.00	1.002	1.14	1.00	0.892	4.49	1.00	1.138	10.97	1.00
Education												
Ability at 11	0.007	5.86	50.18	0.009	2.11	44.27	0.004	2.80	47.68	0.004	3.29	44.92
O-levels	0.015	0.37	0.32	0.074	0.54	0.44	0.103	2.15	0.33	0.065	1.97	0.36
A-Levels	0.072	1.32	0.12	-0.074	-0.25	0.05	0.212	3.07	0.09	0.222	3.57	0.06
Diploma	0.273	5.72	0.19	0.172	0.89	0.14	0.346	5.53	0.21	0.603	13.40	0.15
Degree	0.355	6.75	0.21	0.612	3.09	0.12	0.553	7.86	0.12	0.766	10.80	0.06
Experience												
Years employed since 23	0.103	4.98	7.60	0.005	0.10	6.85	0.047	3.95	6.69	0.038	4.77	5.33
Years in this job	0.051	1.96	7.85	0.031	2.00	4.38	0.015	4.18	6.22	0.009	1.77	3.41
Others												
Father social class 1 or 2	0.067	2.12	0.25	0.122	0.87	0.28	0.093	2.21	0.22	0.074	1.94	0.18
Southeast	0.062	1.86	0.20	0.420	2.71	0.16	0.111	2.38	0.15	0.096	2.65	0.16
λ	0.034	0.96	1.13	-0.143	0.45	2.46	-0.026	0.23	1.46	-0.303	3.77	1.16
Log wage			1.86			1.47			1.69			1.39
Adj R^2	0.285			0.369			0.393			0.455		
n	631			43			420			655		
F	26.090			3.460			28.117			53.351		

All the statistically significant coefficients have the expected signs, but the selection term is significant only for MRC childless women who work full-time. The break in the coefficients of women with different employment status but equal parental status suggests that women cannot escape the low pay of part-time work by not having children. It is the type of job done, rather than her parental status, which makes a woman badly paid. This conclusion is confirmed by table 6.4, which uses the decompositions in (6.1) and (6.3) to isolate the major sources of the full-time/part-time pay gap. Its essential conclusions are summarized in figure 6.1. This table highlights a variety of interesting results.

Table 6.4 is divided horizontally into two blocks: one for each cohort. The MRC block deals with the pay differential between women full-timers and part-timers aged nearly 32 in 1977/8. The NCDS block likewise applies to 33-year-olds in 1991. Within each block there are two panels: description in the smaller panels at the top and analysis beneath. The descriptive panels report the absolute levels of each log wage, and in the top right-hand cell, the difference to be accounted for. These panels also show the sample sizes on which these means were calculated, and the subsample in each case who were mothers. The sample numbers of childless women may be inferred by subtraction. There are not very many of them among part-timers.[8]

In the analysis of each block, the second column, top row, repeats the grand-total raw differential from the top right-hand corner of the top panel. Looking down the first three rows of the analysis panel, we see the decomposition of the wage gap into that occurring within childless women, within mothers, and between them. This follows the formula of decomposition (6.1), which requires the weights, g^f, $(1 - g^f)$, and $(g^f - g^p)$. These are shown in the last column. In the first column of these three rows are the three components (thus weighted), but without any further decomposition as to how far the differentials are due to differences in productive characteristics and parameters. These are shown in columns two and three following decomposition (6.3). The parameter gap in the composition row represents the weighted difference between intercepts in the sub-equations, and the difference in characteristics reflects the different human capital composition of the two subsamples.

The contribution of particular human capital variables is shown separately at the bottom of each block: ability and education as being characteristics mainly acquired before motherhood, and experience as being particularly likely to have been affected by it. The experience row for example, combines the terms in the fitted wage associated with experience

Table 6.4
Decomposition of full-time and part-time pay differentials for women according to motherhood status

	MRC		
	Full-timers	Part-timers	Difference
Mean log wage	0.375	0.048	0.328
n^a	275	310	
of whom mothers	124	279	
	Total	Attributes[b]	Parameters	Weights
Average differential	0.336	0.165	0.171	
Within nonmothers	0.188	0.153	0.036	0.55
Within mothers	0.100	−0.014	0.114	0.45
Composition effect	0.048	0.027	0.022	0.45
Particular components[c] of which due to:				
ability	0.082	0.009	0.073	
education	0.150	0.106	0.044	
experience[d]	0.080	0.005	0.075	

	NCDS		
	Full-timers	Part-timers	Difference
Mean log wage	1.791	1.399	0.392
n	1,051	698	
of whom mothers	420	655	
	Total	Attributes[b]	Parameters	Weights
Average differential	0.392	0.261	0.136	
Within nonmothers	0.234	0.083	0.151	0.60
Within mothers	0.117	0.067	0.050	0.40
Composition effect	0.041	0.111	−0.065	0.54
Particular components[c] of which due to:				
ability	0.107	0.024	0.083	
education	0.021	0.067	−0.046	
experience[d]	0.353	0.164	0.189	

Notes:
a. Unweighted number of observations.
b. Means differences in each subsample weighted by parameters of part-timers, taken from tables 6.2 and 6.3.
c. Does not sum to total as a portion due to other factors such as region is not shown.
d. Includes service with current employer.

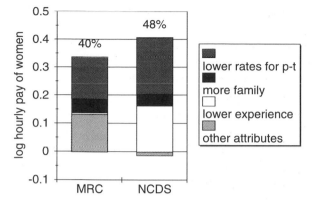

Figure 6.1
Family as source of full- to part-time gap

and tenure from each subsample. It assesses how much they contribute to the predicted differences in average full-time and part-time wages (0.080 for MRC, 0.353 for NCDS). This is shown in white in figure 6.1, bringing out its increasing importance over time. The next columns show how much of this is attributed to differences in human capital and how much to differential returns on that, given the weights adapted for decomposition (6.3) discussed below.

Table 6.4 shows that of the 0.328 log differential found in 1978 for the MRC, only 0.048 was due to more maternal responsibility among part-timers. This is the "composition effect," plotted in black in figure 6.1. The importance of this component appears even smaller by 1991, when it accounted for only 0.041 of the 0.392 gap. It also shows that the penalty to part-time work (i.e., the parameter gap) has declined from just over half (0.171) to just over a third of the gap (0.136).[9] This is despite the fact that the pay differential between women working part-time and their full-time counterparts has increased over the 1980s.

This suggests that in 1991 a larger component of the full-time/part-time gap could be accounted for by the differences in human capital. However, there is also a striking difference in the returns to experience enjoyed by the NCDS full-timers and part-timers respectively. The extent of this differential treatment (of 0.189 in log wages) exceeds the total parameter gap, suggesting that the part-timers receive better returns on some of the other variables in the equation (e.g., education, living in the Southeast). The existence of this differential in the returns to experience could reflect differences in on-the-job training between part-time and full-time workers.

Thus it may be interpreted as a signal of statistical discrimination on the part of the employers.

Table 6.4 also locates the existence of premia to full-time work in both cohorts. This is enjoyed by all women irrespective of whether they have children, although in 1978 it was larger for mothers than for other women (0.114 versus 0.036), while the opposite was true in 1991 (0.050 versus 0.151). The composition of the group accounts for very little of the parameter differential between women working full-time and their part-time counterparts in MRC (0.022) and indeed acts in the opposite direction in NCDS (-0.065). For the 1958 cohort, however, composition is a major component of that part of the differential explained by the workers' attributes (0.111 out of 0.261).

The overall conclusion of table 6.4 and figure 6.1 is that in neither cohort do family responsibilities—as we have measured them—explain the low pay of women employed part-time. The education component of the full-time/part-time gap has declined over time mainly as a result of smaller differences in educational achievement of the NCDS part-timers and the full-timers. Experience, on the other hand, plays a much larger role in NCDS than in MRC. This is due to two factors: (1) the increased disparity in the average length of work experience for full-timers and part-timers, and (2) the much higher remuneration to experience enjoyed by the full-timers (i.e., parameter gap). Finally, it is worth noting that the increase over time in the weight of the "composition effect" $(g^f - g^p)$ reflects an increase in the tendency for childless women to concentrate in full-time jobs.

What Accounts for the Family Gap?

Tables 6.5 and 6.6 provide material to answer our second question: whether the part-time nature of the jobs done by the majority of mothers explains the lower average wage paid to mothers. These tables differ slightly from tables 6.2 and 6.3 because we are able to accept some common parameters for this exercise. Tests for common models within each employment status reject common slope coefficients for mothers and nonmothers only for MRC part-time workers.[10]

The estimations of the earnings equations for the MRC and NCDS cohorts are presented in tables 6.5 and 6.6 respectively. All the coefficients have the expected signs. The insignificant coefficients of the childless intercept for the NCDS cohort and for the MRC members working full-time

Table 6.5
Earnings equations for the MRC cohort in 1978 (maternal status within employment status)

| | Part-timers | | | | | | Full-timers | | | |
| | Mothers | | | Childless women | | | | | Means | |
Variables	Parameters	t-values	Means	Parameters	t-values	Means	Parameters	t-values	Mothers	Childless
Constant	−0.404	2.53	1.00	−0.851	0.64	1.00	0.164	0.56		
If childless							−0.351	1.45		
Woman's education										
Ability at 11	0.003	1.10	50.00	−0.018	2.19	51.71	0.003	0.97	54.01	54.35
O-levels	0.060	1.15	0.25	0.342	2.56	0.25	0.246	3.53	0.27	0.34
A-levels	0.122	1.47	0.07	0.738	2.97	0.09	0.417	4.41	0.12	0.13
Diploma	0.643	4.43	0.02	−0.488	0.98	0.02	0.515	5.12	0.11	0.10
Degree	0.719	3.71	0.01	0.600	1.88	0.05	0.788	5.86	0.00	0.11
Experience										
Years employed, 26–32	0.002	0.13	3.28	−0.019	0.48	5.06	0.034	1.79	4.12	5.44
Years in this job	0.028	2.20	2.16	−0.017	0.65	3.14	0.011	1.47	2.61	5.46
Others										
Father social class 1 or 2	0.013	0.19	0.10	0.131	0.64	0.15	0.041	0.56	0.20	0.21
Southeast	0.017	0.37	0.21	0.107	0.88	0.22	0.078	1.39	0.18	0.32
Selection terms										
λ	0.224	1.53	0.87	0.863	1.72	2.19	−0.294	1.88	1.46	1.08
If childless							0.236	1.42		
Log wage			0.04			0.15			0.49	0.27
Adj R^2	0.208			0.588			0.341			
n	279			31			269			
F	8.297			5.171			12.540			

a. The data are weighted.

Table 6.6
Earnings equations for the 1958 cohort in 1991 (maternal status within employment status)

Variables	Part-timers		Means		Full-timers		Means	
	Parameters	t-values	Mothers	Childless	Parameters	t-values	Mothers	Childless
Constant	1.108	10.87			0.830	4.99		
If childless	−0.679	0.38			−0.101	0.69		
Woman's education								
Ability at 11	0.004	3.59	44.92	44.27	0.006	6.33	47.675	50.18
O-levels	0.067	2.06	0.36	0.44	0.062	2.00	0.33	0.32
A-levels	0.199	3.28	0.64	0.05	0.141	3.31	0.09	0.12
Diploma	0.577	13.14	0.15	0.14	0.316	8.42	0.21	0.19
Degree	0.748	11.21	0.06	0.12	0.438	10.49	0.12	0.21
Experience								
Years employed, 26–32	0.038	4.80	5.33	6.85	0.065	6.72	6.69	7.60
Years in this job	0.010	2.20	3.41	4.38	0.009	4.29	6.22	7.85
Others								
Father social class 1 or 2	0.072	1.95	0.18	0.28	0.078	3.07	0.22	0.25
Southeast	0.115	3.24	0.16	0.16	0.078	2.87	0.15	0.20
Selection terms								
λ	−0.286	3.61	1.16	2.46	−0.061	0.62	1.46	1.13
If childless	0.249	0.84			0.113	1.12		
Log wage			1.39	1.47			1.86	1.69
Adj R^2	0.436				0.358			
n	698				1,051			
F	45.992				49.690			

imply that mothers and childless women share a common intercept as well as common coefficients.[11]

The results of tables 6.5 and 6.6 suggest that within each employment status, there is no "family gap" beyond that attributable exclusively to differences in average human capital characteristics. This conclusion is summarized in table 6.7. This has the same structure and logic as table 6.4. However, here we decompose the difference between the pay of mothers and other women, who are subdivided into groups of full-timers and part-timers. The weights are now defined as in decomposition (6.4). Since there were no significant parameter differences between mothers and non-mothers within NCDS subsamples, the "parameter gap" column represents only the part-time intercept in the pooled model. The other entries are zero.

The first point to note in table 6.7 and figure 6.2 is that the absolute value of the crude "family gap" is almost unchanged between cohorts. It was 0.331 in the log wage in 1978 and it had declined slightly to 0.327 in 1991 (around 39% of mothers' pay in both years). This is despite the advent in the 1980s of family-friendly employment policies designed to support the combination of motherhood and employment alongside equal opportunities policies.[12] However, the relative magnitude of the differences in characteristics and the parameter gap have changed considerably. In 1978 the pay gap between mothers and childless women was almost entirely explained by differences in human capital, and the parameter gap was very small. In 1991 difference in human capital accounted for just over 69% of the pay gap between mothers and childless women. This is not the only difference.

In 1978 around 26% (0.119) of the differential between childless women and mothers was due to the "composition effect" (shown in black in figure 6.2), which reflects the greater proportion of mothers in part-time jobs. By 1991 this had grown to 0.160 (49% of the differential). In 1978 the major part of the composition term was explained by differences in human capital attributes. By 1991 the difference in characteristics had dropped to just over a third of the "composition effect" (0.058 out of 0.160, or 36%).

The pay differential between mothers working full-time and other full-timers remains the main source of the family gap in both cohorts, although its relative importance is reduced in NCDS. In both cohorts this component of the pay gap is entirely explained by the higher stock of human capital held by the full-timers who have not (yet) had children. It is worth noting, though, that the work experience component of the human

Table 6.7
Accounting for the family gap in the MRC and NCDS cohorts

	MRC			
	Childless women	Mothers	Difference	
Mean log wage	0.431	0.100	0.331	
n^a	181	398		
of whom part-time	31	279		
	Total	Attributes[b]	Parameters	Weights
Average differential	0.331	0.235	0.096	
Within full-timers	0.186	0.186	0.000	0.47
Within part-timers	0.019	−0.049	0.075	0.53
Composition effect	0.119	0.098	0.021	0.52
Particular components[c]				
of which due to:				
ability	0.172	0.006	0.167	
education	0.057	0.132	0.007	
experience[d]	0.041	0.041	0.000	

	NCDS			
	Childless women	Mothers	Difference	
Mean log wage	1.836	1.508	0.327	
n	674	1075		
of whom part-time	43	655		
	Total	Attributes[b]	Parameters	Weights
Average differential	0.327	0.226	0.101	
Within full-timers	0.163	0.163	0.000	0.94
Within part-timers	0.005	0.005	0.000	0.06
Composition effect	0.160	0.058	0.101	0.52
Particular components[c]				
of which due to:				
ability	0.158	0.014	0.144	
education	−0.058	0.079	−0.137	
experience[d]	0.512	0.129	0.383	

Notes:
a. Unweighted number of observations.
b. Means differences within each subsample weighted by parameters relevant to mothers (where different) in tables 6.5 and 6.6.
c. Does not sum to total as a portion due to other factors such as region is not shown.
d. Includes service with current employer.

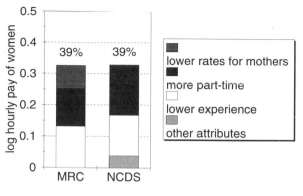

Figure 6.2
Sources of family pay gap

capital differential may itself be the result of motherhood. Figure 6.2 shows its increasing importance in accounting for the lower relative pay of the average mother. Finally pay differentials within full-timers are lower in 1991 than in 1978.[13]

The overall conclusion is that for both cohorts the concentration of mothers in low-paid part-time jobs goes a long way toward explaining the "family gap." Indeed, among full-timers, in neither cohort have we found evidence of the direct "penalty to motherhood" that one might expect if Becker's hypothesis about limited effort applied (Becker 1985). What we have found—in common with previous studies—is ample evidence of a "penalty to part-time" whether or not a woman has children. The other major source of the family gap among full-timers is the comparatively low stock of human capital—mainly work experience—held by the mothers as compared to childless women.

An additional finding is that the relative role of ability, education, and experience has changed considerably in magnitude in the two cohorts. Ability explained about half of the differential in both cases. Education explained 42% of the family gap faced by the MRC women, but is a negative term for the NCDS women, suggesting that education favors the mothers who are in the labor market. This is because, though their educational level is on average lower, their returns to this factor are higher. On the other hand, the experience component has become far more important due to a very sharp increase in the differential reward it receives among the two groups of women.

Are the "wages of motherhood" better in the 1990s? The evidence in table 6.7 suggests not. Unadjusted, the family gap was much the same in 1991 as in 1978. The part of the gap that could be accounted for by mothers being less educated and able than childless women has fallen.

The pay penalties to motherhood that are most likely to reflect its consequences rather than its antecedents (and anticipation) are lost employment experience, the impact of more part-time jobs, and any parameter differences expressing different rewards to given attributes to women with and without children. In the two samples the pay consequences of motherhood, thus defined, are as follows:

	MRC	NCDS
Lost experience	0.041	0.129
Extra part-time	0.119	0.160
Lower rewards	0.075	net zero
	0.235	0.289

The part of the family gap accounted for by the indirect consequences of motherhood increased. These estimates of the "wages of motherhood" correspond to others made by Joshi and Newell (1989, table 4.3) for the MRC cohort:

	Age	
	26	32
Work experience	0.081	0.045
Part-time	0.041	0.056
Occupational downgrading	0.048	0.054
Nonsignificant residual	0.017	0.016
	0.154	0.143

In the model used in this case, job characteristics were also controlled for, and parameters were not significantly different between mothers and others in either 1972 or 1978. The inclusion of job characteristics here must be the major reason why the earlier estimate for MRC at age 32 involved little "direct effect," or parameter difference. Any net downgrading in occupational status since age 18 was treated as a possible consequence of motherhood, reflecting the well-known phenomenon of occupational downgrading after childbearing (see Joshi and Newell 1987; Joshi and Hinde 1993; Dex 1987; Martin and Roberts 1984). In our models, any effect of occupational downgrading of returnees is subsumed in that of lost labor-market experience and taking part-time work.[14]

These results are not dissimilar from what other British and U.S. evidence suggest. For the United Kingdom, Dolton and Makepeace (1987) found a negative effect of children on the wage of female graduates, but Harkness (1996) finds that the effect of children on wages works predominantly through the reduction in work experience. For the United States, Waldfogel (1997b) undertook a similar study of two cohorts, using data from the National Longitudinal Survey of Young Women (NLS-YW) and the National Longitudinal Survey of Youth (NLSY). Her sample from the NLS-YW cohort was on average age 30 in 1980; the NLSY cohort was on average age 30 in 1991 (They are almost the exact contemporaries of our cohorts.) She found that, although the gender pay gap narrowed sharply over the period 1980 to 1991 in the United States, the gap between mothers and other women widened. Nonmothers earned 72% of men's average pay in 1980, 12 percentage points ahead of mothers at 60% of men's pay. In 1991, nonmothers earned 95% of men's pay, 20 percentage points ahead of mothers at 75% of men's pay. Not surprisingly, she found that family status (the negative returns women receive for having children, as opposed to the positive returns men receive for being married and having children) accounted for a large share of the gender gap in both cohorts, and a share that grew in importance over the decade: 36% in 1980 and 53% in 1991. Similar results are found by Neumark and Korenman (1994) using NLS-YW when the potential endogeneity of experience and tenure are fully accounted for by means of instrumental variable techniques. Wood et al. (1993) point to the existence of a considerable penalty to motherhood (one-fourth to one-third of the earnings gap) among the fairly homogeneous group of graduates of the University of Michigan Law School.

However, none of these studies looks explicitly at the potential effects of part time work on the family gap, as mothers are much less concentrated in part-time work in the United States than they are in Britain. In the NLSY cohort, for example, less than a quarter of all women are working part-time, a rate about three times higher than that of men. By contrast, in NCDS 33% of women are working part-time, a rate over thirty times higher than that of men. The relative importance of the "composition effect" is therefore expected to be much smaller.

Does Maternity Leave Protect Earning Power?

The pivotal role of employment experience in explaining the family gap leads us to question whether our initial specification of the experience effect adequately captured the loss of expertise and training resulting from absence from the labor market following childbearing. We also wondered whether the striking difference in remuneration for mothers and childless women in NCDS may not reflect differential effort and job commitment among mothers.

We explore the matter further by analyzing two distinct groups within the NCDS mothers: the "maternity leavers" who have employment continuity around their first childbirth, and those whose work histories were interrupted for more than a year.[15] Well over half the NCDS mothers in full-time employment fell into the group that is presumed (but not known) to have taken maternity leave. NCDS women had occasion to benefit from the introduction of statutory maternity leave in 1976, although not from the relaxation, in 1994, of its job tenure and hours conditions.

After a series of tests for common models within cohorts, we allow only for structural differences in the parameters of the earnings equations for part-timers and full-timers, including different intercepts for childless women, "maternity leavers," and other mothers. The results of estimating the earnings equations are presented in table 6.8. All the coefficients have the expected sign and most of them are significantly different from zero. The insignificance of the "maternity leaver" and "childless" intercepts for part-timers suggests that all women working part-time share the same intercept. They also share the same significantly negative selection term.

Among full-timers, on the other hand, maternity leavers and childless women have an intercept that is significantly higher than that of other women, but not significantly different from one another. There are several possible explanations for the lower intercept of mothers with interrupted work histories. Childless women and maternity leavers might have higher wages than other mothers because they differ in some unobserved attribute such as commitment or effort. Alternatively the difference might be due to mothers who interrupt their careers being penalized in some way that we do not observe (e.g., lower training, lower chance of promotion, poorer job match) in the labor market.

The significantly positive selection term for full-timers appears to be counteracted by the negative coefficients of the interactions between λ and the dummies for "maternity leaver" and "childless." The positive selection term would support the argument of those who identify mothers working full-time as a particularly motivated group with more earning potential than their childless counterparts. They definitely would need to be well paid to be able to afford formal child care (Ward et al. 1996). But the interaction suggests this does not apply if they are "maternity leavers."

Table 6.8
Earnings equations for the 1958 cohort in 1991: Maternity leavers, other mothers, and childless women

Variables	Part-timers		Full-timers	
	Parameters	t-values	Parameters	t-values
Earnings equation				
Constant	1.240	10.35	0.458	1.54
If maternity leaver	0.034	0.14	0.998	2.88
If childless	−0.311	0.48	0.643	2.15
Woman's education				
Ability at 11	0.003	3.14	0.006	6.19
O-levels	0.066	2.04	0.058	1.87
A-levels	0.182	3.05	0.110	2.56
Diploma	0.562	11.67	0.295	7.96
Degree	0.667	10.27	0.405	9.44
Experience				
Years employed, 26–33	0.002	3.52	0.002	3.86
Years in this job	0.010	2.23	0.010	4.82
Others				
Father social class 1 or 2	0.067	1.79	0.074	2.91
Southeast	0.109	3.08	0.079	2.91
Selection terms				
λ	−0.250	3.01	0.277	1.84
If maternity leaver	0.067	0.44	−0.505	2.73
If childless	0.249	0.90	−0.246	1.58
Log wage				
Childless women	1.471		1.861	
Maternity leavers	1.582		1.787	
Other mothers	1.284		1.506	
Adj R^2	0.440		0.349	
n	698		1,051	
F	40.121		41.156	

The lower λ of this group might reflect a sort of compensating wage differential, so that the privilege of being in jobs where continuous employment is easier and more secure is acquired at the cost of lower wages.

Finally, we note the striking similarity of the "maternity leavers" and the nonmothers. Not only is the hypothesis of the coefficients being different for the two groups of women strongly rejected, but the intercepts for not having children and for being a maternity leaver are well within each other's standard errors.

The result confirms previous findings by Waldfogel (1993, 1995) on an earlier version of the same data set and on American data.[16] In the contemporary NLSY cohort, women with two children have wages 10–12% lower than other women, even after controlling for education and work experience. However, women who had access to maternity leave coverage and used it to maintain employment continuity over their most recent birth had wages 10–12% higher than other women. Thus, in this cohort, being a "maternity leaver" cancelled out the pay penalties of motherhood. This result is comparable to that reported above, where NCDS "maternity leavers" have essentially the same earnings function as childless women, in contrast to women who have had children but did not maintain employment continuity. The finding means that the pay penalty to motherhood we have detected among otherwise identical full-timers only affects those who do not maintain continuous employment over their first child's birth.

However, this does not imply that the gender gap has been eliminated for those women who maintain uninterrupted work histories as full-time workers. Although the nonmothers and the maternity leavers working full-time are better paid than other mothers, they are still paid considerably less than men employed full-time with the same characteristics. The comparison of men with maternity leavers and childless women, presented in table 6.9, reveals that although they receive the same rewards for the productivity-related characteristics,[17] nonmothers and maternity leavers working full-time face an unexplained wage penalty of 18% and 23% respectively (0.163 and 0.203 in log terms). This penalty exceeds the unadjusted gap between the wages of these women (0.113 in the case of childless women, and 0.187 in the case of maternity leavers). This occurs because these groups of women have unusually high endowments, which are being compared to the average for all men.

This result confirms earlier findings by Wood et al. (1993) for graduates of the University of Michigan Law School. Their sample includes men and women lawyers fifteen years after leaving law school. These individuals

Table 6.9
Earnings equations for the 1958 cohort full-timers in 1991: Maternity leavers, childless women, and men pooled

Variables	Full-timers	
	Parameters	t-values
Earnings equation		
Constant	0.752	16.45
If maternity leaver	−0.203	11.67
If childless	−0.163	12.25
Education		
Ability at 11	0.005	11.37
O-levels	0.088	5.59
A-Levels	0.157	8.61
Diploma	0.301	16.39
Degree	0.451	22.82
Experience		
Years employed, 26−33	0.099	17.21
Years in this job	0.005	4.85
Others		
Father social class 1 or 2	0.025	1.83
Southeast	0.170	12.70
Log wage		
Childless women	1.861	
Maternity leavers	1.787	
Men	1.975	
Adj R²	0.340	
N	4,573	
F	212.348	

are thus somewhat older than those in our samples, and much more homogeneous in terms of the their human capital characteristics and of the tendency for these highly educated mothers to take short career breaks around childbearing. Nevertheless, the results are remarkably similar to ours. Their highly educated and highly committed mothers earn no less than childless women, but both earn only 60% as much as their male counterparts.

Table 6.10 summarizes the pay gap between men and employed mothers in NCDS. Figure 6.3 compares the wages of men and mothers at two points in the history of the 1946 cohort (estimated by Joshi 1991) and age 33 for NCDS (derived from tables 6.7 and 6.9). The overall gap

Table 6.10
Accounting for the gap between men and mothers

| | Hourly wage relative to mothers' actual | | |
| | MRC | | NCDS |
	Age 26 1972	Age 32 1977–78	Age 33 1991
Actual pay of mothers in paid work	100	100	100
Wage mothers would receive if motherhood had no pay consequences	120	122	120
Wage mothers would receive if paid as men	176	134	122
Wage mothers would receive if motherhood had no pay consequences and women were paid men's rates	190	156	141
Actual wage of men	200	181	160

Source: Columns 1 and 2: Joshi 1991; column 3: table 6.9.

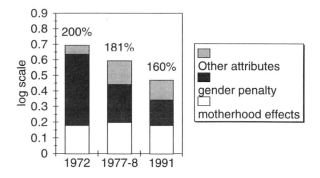

Figure 6.3
Sources of pay gap: men to mothers
Source: Cohort studies.

narrowed from men's pay being double the mothers' in 1972, through an 81% excess in 1977/78 to 60% in 1991. The pay differentials attributed to the direct and indirect effects of motherhood were virtually unchanged, or around 20% of mother's pay. What brought the two wages closer together was a closing of the gender premium over a period when equal pay laws came into force. The other components plotted in figure 6.3 show little change.

If we perform the thought experiment that mothers suffered no adverse pay consequences of motherhood, they would still have been paid substantially less than men because of their different initial human capital endowment and differential rates at which it is remunerated. The latter can be thought of as the pay penalties of sex rather than motherhood. For the 1946 cohort, these were substantially more important parts of the gap than motherhood. For NCDS the consequences of motherhood and gender are about the same. It would appear that differences in pay between men and mothers have still not been reduced to those due to domestic responsibility.

Conclusions

Our results suggest that it is the concentration of mothers in part-time jobs that leads to their low wage. The alternative view, that the low pay of part-timers is accounted for by many of them having children, receives less support. Although we found some evidence of unequal treatment of mothers among MRC part-timers, we find little support for mothers receiving consistently adverse rates of pay, all else equal. Differences in family responsibilities between women working part-time and full-time explain only 14% in a 40% differential in the MRC study and 10% in a 48% differential in NCDS. The earnings differential between mothers and childless women has not declined over time; the component due to mothers' greater tendency to work part-time has increased considerably. In the 1946 cohort it represented around a third of a 39% differential, but it had grown to just under half of the differential by 1991.

Reasons why motherhood might reduce pay include an impact on productivity or labor-market leverage, or discrimination, probably "statistical." Our finding of the relative importance of part-time employment as an explanation of mothers' low pay (rather than motherhood cutting pay across the board) reduces the plausibility of the story of the low productivity associated with domestic responsibilities. Becker (1981) and Hakim (1996), for example, maintain that it is the low effort or motivation in the paid sphere of women with children at home that leads to low pay through low productivity. This would imply that mothers who chose part-time jobs were of a specially uncommitted type. Our tests of selection process have found few otherwise unobserved peculiarities in the NCDS subsamples.

We are led to several alternative interpretations. The first refers to the lower elasticity of supply of part-time workers, which is supported by some of the findings in chapter 5, for example, the shorter travel-to-work time of part-timers. The second refers to the possible nonlinearity of the wage-hour locus that could result, for example, from "warm-up" effects, which may reduce the ratio of effective to recorded hours of work for part-timers relative to full-timers. The general association of part-time jobs with domestic ties may also help to create statistical discrimination against all part-timers, but such a perception does not seem to afflict all full-timers with children.

We enquired into the specific effect of employment interruption at the crucial juncture of entry to motherhood. We tested whether mothers who have gone back to work directly after (what we presume was) their statutory maternity leave were paid better than other mothers. We find that within each employment status, the returns to human capital characteristics for "maternity leavers" are not significantly different from those of other mothers.

The striking similarity of the "maternity leavers" and the women with no children means that the pay penalty to motherhood we have detected among otherwise identical full-timers only affects those who do not maintain continuous employment over their first child's birth. However, this is not to say that childless women (and women who took maternity leave) are treated like men. They face a strong gender penalty that more than offsets the higher level of their average endowment. For the average mother in NCDS, the effect of the gender penalty is about as much again as the direct and indirect pay consequences of motherhood.

For the 1946 cohort, gender had been the dominant component of mothers' low pay relative to men. Family responsibilities contributed only marginally to the explanation of the low pay of part-timers in the 1946 cohort. This is despite their being observed in a period when family-friendly employment practice had hardly been heard of, and most having had their first child before the introduction of statutory maternity leave in 1976. Factors such as the mothers' increased likelihood of working part-time and their lower work experience compared to the childless reduced their pay, but we detected no additional penalty. The relative role of parental status as a source of the part-time/full-time gap had decreased further in 1991. This could perhaps be attributed to the arrival of family-friendly practices and the fact that maternity leave legislation had been in place for most of the childbearing years of the 1958 cohort.

The fact that full-time employees who took maternity leave were more or less protected from the adverse pay consequences of motherhood means that is unlikely that the family-friendly employment policies and the lower wages of mothers came all in one package from certain employers. Our results are more likely to reflect the patchy spread of the family-friendly employers, and to indicate benefits to be anticipated from the extension of maternity rights after 1994.

When all else is held constant, motherhood does not appear to lead to one woman being much worse paid than another with no children. This approach, comparing women, cannot allow for the fact that all women, especially at this age, may be perceived as potential if not actual mothers. Impending motherhood, whether or not the anticipation is correct, may still be part of the story if it helps to generate statistical discrimination between men and all women. The evidence from some women in these cohorts is that it would be wrong to presume that motherhood necessarily lowers a woman's capacity for paid work. Discrimination on this presumption would be inefficient as well as inequitable.

The first part of this chapter draws together the main findings of the previous chapters and compares them with other findings from the 1946 cohort. The second part discusses their implications for policy.

An Overview of Findings

This study is one of the first to explore and exploit a major data resource on the passage into adulthood of a cohort born in 1958 and residing in the United Kingdom: the fifth sweep of the National Child Development Study. This was carried out in 1991, when the cohort members were 33 years old. In particular, this is one of the first analyses of the cohort members' rates of pay at 33, and of how these vary by and within gender. The study is doubly unique because we have been able to make a comparison with those emerging from the equivalent sweep of the MRC National Survey of Health and Development. This was carried out in 1977–78, when the members of that cohort were approaching 32.

The timing of the relevant sweeps of the two cohorts, on either side of the 1980s, is ideal for an analysis of gender wage differentials. The 1980s saw continuing changes in traditions concerning the formation of families and the division of labor within them. The educational attainments of young women caught up with those of men, reducing gender differences in human capital. Substantial changes in the legislative framework in which women's employment takes place were implemented in the 1970s (as described in chapter 1), and a tentative move toward "family-friendly" employment practice gained some impetus in the 1980s.

Data from the New Earnings Survey for full-time employees of all ages, presented in chapter 3, show that the lead of average men's wages over women's had already come down to 38% (from 58% in 1970 before the

Equal Pay Act). Convergence of men's and women's hourly rates continued over the 1980s. By 1991 the ratio was 28%. We asked whether this
trend reflected continual improvement in the treatment of women in the
labor market. The narrowing of the gap could simply result from gender
differences in the accumulation of human capital. Relative to men, NCDS
women, particularly if working full-time, were much better endowed with
educational qualifications and employment experience than their MRC
counterparts. Women's participation in employment, especially in full-
time jobs, had gone up at age 32–33, and so had their employment experience (and the average age at motherhood). On the other hand, in the
same period disparity widened in the productive characteristics held by
women.

The existence of two highly comparable cohort studies, so conveniently
spaced, provides a unique opportunity to go behind the superficial indicators of change. We can see what brought men's and women's wages
together—and what still kept them apart—over a period of thirteen
crucial years. In 1978, equal pay, sex discrimination, and employment
protection laws had only recently been implemented. By 1991 they had
been operational for a decade and a half. They had been amended and
were fairly well established. The comparison of the pay gaps in 1978 and
1991 enabled us to monitor the effectiveness of equal opportunities legislation, its progress and limitations.

Although the cohort studies have data on only a narrow age band, their
experience is not dissimilar to that of employees of all ages in the New
Earnings Survey. The cohort studies also reflect the generalized widening
of earnings differentials experienced in the British labor market over the
1980s. This is particularly evident in the growing gap between the wages
of women employed full-time and part-time.

The focus of our analysis is on trends and determinants of wage differentials between men and women and, among the latter, between full-time
and part-time workers. We use the evidence collected in the two cohorts
to examine in the first instance how far the convergence of men's and
women's wages that occurred over the 1980s in full-time jobs reflects an
improvement in the treatment of the sexes, rather than the convergence
of their productive endowment. We then move on to analyze along the
same lines the determinants of the trends in the full-time/part-time pay
gap among women. In combination these two gaps reflect the overall
gender gap between men in full-time employment and all women.

The cohort studies provide detailed data on productive endowments,
such as individual work experience, service with the same employer,

schooling, ability, and aspirations. They are therefore particularly suitable to the type of analysis we have conducted.

The first investigation of the determinants of wage differentials in this study (chapter 4) controlled for differences in human capital characteristics in a regression analysis. An alternative estimate of a human capital model for NCDS is presented in chapter 5. This then expands to incorporate additional explanatory variables reflecting the characteristics of the employer, the type of job, the occupation level, and the extent of segregation in the relevant occupation. Responsibility for children is assessed as another potential influence on wage levels, in chapter 6.

Tables 7.1 and 7.2 bring together some of the summary findings from these analyses. Table 7.1 and figures 7.1 and 7.2 represent the wage differentials in terms of logarithms, and table 7.2 reports them as percentages of the lower wage being compared.

The first column of tables 7.1 and 7.2 offers estimates for the overall wage gap between men and all women, full- and part-timers. This is a weighted combination of the differentials shown in the next two columns, in the case of estimates derived from regressions reported in this book. The rows in each panel split the crude pay gap into parameter and attribute components as in table 5.5. These tables have some entries in common with the summary of analyses in chapter 5. They also draw on comparable material from other chapters and our previous study of the 1946 cohort (Joshi and Newell 1989). The last column reports the sample size used in each estimate, for men, women employed full-time, and women employed part-time separately. These numbers vary across cohorts and different specifications within cohorts because of variation in missing information and the way we have handled it. The main features of the overall comparison made in column 1 are plotted in figures 7.1 and 7.2.

The wage differential between men and all women was around 60% in 1978 for the 1946 cohort. By the time the 1958 cohort reached 33, in 1991, it had dropped to somewhere between 37% and 40% (depending on the sample used) (table 7.2). The drop in the crude gender gap was even larger when the analysis was limited to full-timers. Among this group of workers, the gap halved over the period (from 36% to 18%, or to 20% if the other sample is used). The pay gap between women in full- and part-time jobs had changed in the opposite direction.

Regression analysis permits a partitioning of observed pay gaps into a part that is accounted for by explanatory variables and one that reflects differences in parameters across different groups of workers. We refer to this parameter component as the "gender premium," the "full-time gender

Table 7.1
Summary of log wage gaps in the 1958 and 1946 cohorts

				Sample numbers
Model and year of data	Men: all women	Men: women full-time	Women full-time: part-time	Men FT women PT women
Human capital				
1977–78, Age 31–32				
Total differential	0.456	—	—	918
Parameter gap	0.281	—	—	227
Gap in characteristics	0.177	—	—	245
(Joshi and Newell 1989, table 3.2)				
Total differential	0.491	0.305	0.335	1,051
Parameter gap	0.321	0.214	0.193	263
Gap in characteristics	0.170	0.091	0.142	272
(Chapter 4, table 4.5)				
1991, Age 33				
Total differential	0.313	0.167	0.392	3,098
Parameter gap	0.238	0.156	0.220	1,421
Gap in characteristics	0.075	0.011	0.172	847
(Chapter 4, table 4.5)				
Total differential	0.337	0.183	0.419	1,797
Parameter gap	0.244	0.166	0.211	866
Gap in characteristics	0.093	0.017	0.208	504
(Chapter 5, table 5.1)				
Human capital plus job characteristics				
1977–78, Age 31–32				
Total differential	0.456	—	—	918
Parameter gap	0.243	—	—	227
Gap in characteristics	0.214	—	—	245
(Joshi and Newell 1989, table 3.2)				
1991, Age 33				
Total differential	0.337	0.183	0.419	1,797
Parameter gap	0.136	0.114	0.062	866
Gap in characteristics	0.201	0.069	0.357	504
(Chapter 5, table 5.4)				
Human capital plus job characteristics plus parenthood				
1991, Age 33				
Total differential	0.337	0.183	0.419	1,797
Parameter gap	0.123	0.108	0.041	866
Gap in characteristics	0.214	0.075	0.378	504
(Chapter 6, table 6.1)				

Note: The men in these samples virtually all have full-time jobs: 99% in MRC and 100% in NCDS by sample definition.

Table 7.2
Wage Gaps in terms of percentages of the lower rate: 1958 and 1946 cohorts at ages 33 and 32

Model and year of data	Men: all women	Men: women full-time	Women full-time: part-time	Sample numbers Men FT women PT women
Human capital				
1977–78, Age 31–32				
Total differential	57.8	—	—	918
Parameter gap	32.4	—	—	227
Gap in characteristics (Joshi and Newell, table 3.2)	19.4	—	—	245
Total differential	63.4	35.7	39.8	1,051
Parameter gap	37.9	23.9	21.3	263
Gap in characteristics (Chapter 4, table 4.5)	18.5	9.5	15.3	272
1991, Age 33				
Total differential	36.8	18.2	48.0	3,098
Parameter gap	26.9	16.9	24.6	1,421
Gap in characteristics (Chapter 4, table 4.5)	7.8	1.1	18.8	847
Total differential	40.1	20.1	52.0	1,797
Parameter gap	27.6	18.1	23.5	866
Gap in characteristics (Chapter 5, table 5.1)	9.7	1.7	23.1	504
Human capital plus job characteristics				
1977–78, Age 31–32				
Total differential	57.8	—	—	918
Parameter gap	27.5	—	—	227
Gap in characteristics (Joshi and Newell, table 3.2)	23.9	—	—	245
1991, Age 33				
Total differential	40.1	20.1	52.0	1,797
Parameter gap	14.6	12.1	6.4	866
Gap in characteristics (Chapter 5, table 5.5)	22.3	7.1	42.9	504
Human capital plus job characteristics plus parenthood				
1991, Age 33				
Total differential	40.1	20.1	52.0	1,797
Parameter gap	13.1	11.4	4.2	866
Gap in characteristics (Chapter 6, table 6.1)	23.9	7.8	45.9	504

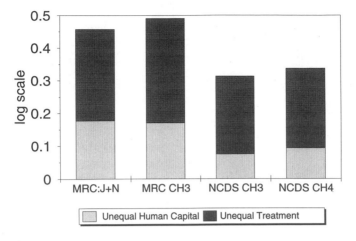

Figure 7.1
Analysis of pay gaps: men to all women

premium," or the "part-time penalty," depending on the groups being compared.

In chapter 4 we found that in the early years of implementation of the Equal Pay Act, the members of the 1946 cohort, then in their early thirties, experienced a gender premium of over one-third of women's pay (38%) after adjusting for differences in mean productivity endowments. This result was not much different from the findings of Joshi and Newell (1989) on the same cohort (a premium of around 32%, out of a sample with a smaller crude differential of 58%). As shown in figure 7.1, comparable estimates for the NCDS in 1991 (panels 3 and 4) are around one-quarter (25% or 28% according to the sample used). A gender premium around one-quarter is still no lower than the estimates for married persons of all ages in 1980 by Wright and Ermisch (1991) and other findings for all women cited in chapter 1, and we found no strong evidence for any improvement over time.

To the extent that parameter differences represent genuine unequal treatment in the labor market, rather than a measure of ignorance, discrimination does not yet seem to be a thing of the past. But, comparing cohorts, its extent appears to be declining over time—by around 9 percentage points (somewhere between 5 and 13 points) of the wages of women in their thirties between 1978 and 1991. Less unequal treatment could be the result of equal opportunities policy, particularly the 1983 Equal Pay Amendment Act, although other trends and transformations in the labor market may also have contributed to (or moderated) its reduction. One such trend, peculiar to this age group, is the relative decline of part-time employment among women employees. There are thus "composition" effects, analogous to those we explore in chapter 6, contributing to the improvement in treatment experienced by the average woman. In 1991 she was more likely to escape the pitfalls of part-time pay.

Contrary to expectations, the declining trend in the gender premium is not as pronounced among full-timers. The unequal treatment component of the gender gap among this group goes down from 21% to somewhere between 17% and 18%. This is marginally below Harkness's estimates for full-time women and men of all ages in 1992–93, 22% in the human capital model. At the same time, the part of the full-time gender gap that is explained by differences in human capital endowment has almost disappeared. This means that among men and women born in 1958 who were in full-time jobs, men's hitherto traditional advantage in educational attainments and experience was minimal. The presumption that on average men are better qualified than their female colleagues appears not to hold any longer for full-timers in this generation (or those following). This is an important finding, as this change may increase employers' interest in conserving the human capital of their employees with practices that help the combination of employment with family responsibilities.

Harkness (1996) also estimates a diminishing attribute component of the gender gap among full-timers of all ages (not including experience) equivalent to 0.068 in 1973, 0.079 in 1984, and 0.025 in 1992. This is not indeed very different from our estimate of a human capital gap of 0.091 in 1978 and 0.011 in 1991 for the single-age cohorts. Thus we have change in a similar direction but of smaller magnitude in the general population. The parameter gaps estimated by Harkness are slightly bigger (40% in 1974, 27% in 1983, 22% in 1992/3), also moving in the same direction.

Figure 7.2 summarizes the result of including further information in our models, as well as human capital, job characteristics, and family responsibilities. These features add little to the explanation of differential pay to men and women, for substantial within-job differences emerge in the dark shaded areas in figure 7.2. They nevertheless represent some contribution and do show some signs of improving over time.

The information on job characteristics adds surprisingly little to the explanation of the full-time gender gap in either cohort. Sorting within the labor market nevertheless contributes to unequal pay. The fact that men and women tend to do different types of jobs confirms the "crowding" hypothesis, and limits the writ of "equal pay for equal work." Allowing for

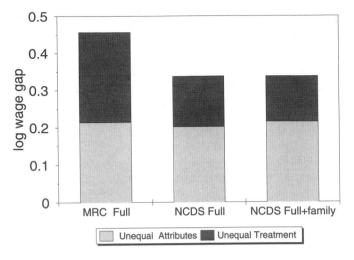

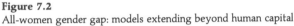

Figure 7.2
All-women gender gap: models extending beyond human capital

characteristics of the firm, job, industry, and occupation leaves an otherwise unexplained gender premium of 12% of women's full-time pay. Our fullest model of hourly pay for full-timers leaves less accounted by differential treatment than the analysis by Dale and Egerton (1997) on NCDS full-timer weekly pay. That model includes more detail on qualifications, and less on job characteristics, and results in a D_f of 20%.

What seems to have changed in the opposite direction is the pay penalty for women's part-time work. The full-timers in MRC average 40% more than part-timers. This gap had grown to around 50% in NCDS. The share of human capital characteristics in explaining this differential had also grown from around two-fifths of the gap to just over half. Job characteristics are more important here. Adding them to the account of the gap between full-timers and part-timers reduces the parameter gap to 6%. Harkness (1996) finds a smaller—even negative—full-time premium among women of all ages in a similar model.

Relevant features of part-time jobs include their low-status occupations, their tendency to be in small private firms, and to involve a shorter journey to work. The latter suggests monopsony may lead to low wages.

The growing gulf between rates of pay for full-time and part-time employment among young women in the 1980s is therefore the result of two factors. The first is the increase in the already marked differences in the average human capital endowments of women in full-time and part-time jobs. The second is a slight increase in the adjusted premium. The latter appears to be part and parcel of a more general tendency for differentials to open up in the labor market, where an increase in unequal treatment of part-timers would not have been surprising. According to Harkness (1996), such an increase occurred between 1974 and 1983, but not thereafter.

Family responsibilities do not appear to be the missing link accounting for the low pay of part-timers. Differences in pay between mothers and other women in 1991 were completely accounted for by human capital characteristics and whether the job was part-time. Being a mother entails no direct pay penalty, beyond the indirect consequences of lost experience and part-time employment for which we make allowance. When the full-timers in 1991 were further subdivided, a pay penalty to motherhood appeared among women who did not take maternity leave. In 1978, allowing for the presence of children in the home did make a difference among part-timers. The bottom panel of tables 7.1 and 7.2 introduce parental status into the full model for NCDS. This modestly increases the still small fraction of the gender pay gap for full-timers (from 7.1% to 7.8%), which is explained. Between the full-timers and part-timers it increased the explained component from 43% to 46%, leaving a part-time penalty of 4%. For both NCDS and MRC cohorts, part-time employment accounts for a good deal of the low pay of mothers, but motherhood does little to explain the low pay of part-timers.

The 1980s saw the advent of a family-friendly agenda for employment practices. They also saw the emergence of a negative premium in full-time pay for some NCDS mothers. This suggests that economic opportunities for women with children had actually deteriorated, at least in some parts of the labor market. The pay penalty specifically for motherhood in NCDS has been narrowed down to those in full-time employment who had a major interruption in their job record around the time of their first birth. Part-timers seem to be more or less uniformly low paid whether or not they have children. Full-timers who had minimized employment interruption at their first child were paid as well as childless women. This is perhaps evidence of the uneven spread of practices facilitating mothers' employment rather than of their ineffectiveness. For those who did take up the maternity leave more often available to this cohort, earning power seems to have been preserved. Neither taking maternity leave nor remaining childless permit women to escape the financial penalty of being female.

To recap: there was still a gender penalty for 33-year-old women in 1991, whatever their position in the labor market. This was more severe for mothers who have full-time jobs, but a broken employment record at the time of their first birth. It was less severe for those who minimized any gap and those who had not (yet) had children. It is even more severe for women employed part-time, if their pay is compared with men employed full-time. As far as labor-market opportunities are concerned, it paid to be born male in 1958 as well as 1946.

This tale of two cohorts does not cover enough of their lives to separate life-cycle, period, and cohort differences definitively. We have concentrated on two snapshots in their history when they are roughly the same age, and even more roughly at the same stage of their life course. This comparison of their wages can be thought of as between cohorts or between periods. The former would involve permanent differences that distinguish one cohort from another, and which might be expected to persist through time. Period factors, however, would affect all age groups simultaneously, and might be reversed.

Our two cohorts certainly differ in their accumulation of human capital. Improvements in this have helped account for the convergence of men's and women's wages in full-time jobs. The process of cohort replacement also produces secular change in the composition of the labor force, contributing to a closing of the wage gap between men and women full-timers of all ages. Among part-timers, the influence of human capital has moved in the other direction. A smaller proportion of women employees in the later cohort were part-time. They were more selected for low human capital, leading to a divergence between sectors alongside the increased inequality within full-timers of each sex.

The continued slow improvement in the treatment of women relative to men in the full-time labor market is a period phenomenon, extending the more dramatic changes around the time the Equal Pay Act was introduced. The widening gulf between full- and part-time wages for women is associated with changes in the structure of employment and labor-market deregulation. It can also be thought of as a sign of the times—a "period effect." It extends to other ages. The arrival of the new Labour government in 1997 increases the prospect of the times changing again.

We have observed a period, up to 1991, when two forces were pulling wage differentials in opposite directions. Equal opportunity policy offered greatest benefits to better-educated full-timers. Deregulation worsened the terms of part-time employment. There are thus differences within cohorts as important as those between them: the integration of well-educated women into the mainstream of full-time employment, and the marginalization of part-timers.

Our analyses reveal signs of discrimination in unequal remuneration in two sets of wage gaps: between men and women employed full-time and between women working full- and part-time. These have been the main focus of the commentary, though they remain in a way unexplained. Though such residual gaps are taken to represent discrimination in the technical literature, they may have arisen in a number of ways. The unequal treatment may not be intentional. It is not necessarily all (or even at all) overt, law-breaking discrimination with malicious intent. Workers may, in theory, be content to accept "compensating differentials" to offset other features of the job. Apart from this, imperfections in the labor market and in employers' knowledge, asymmetry of information and bargaining power, and segregation of occupations can all prevent markets operating to eliminate any differential that is not rewarding variations in personal productivity.

These explanations could all apply to each of the two gaps studied. Each may have arisen from a variety of causes, and we have not been able to reject rigorously any one explanation. Among those we think are important, on the basis of the evidence presented, are vertical occupational segregation and labor-market segmentation. We also point out that part-timers working in local labor markets can face monopsonistic employers who set low wages for a "captive" workforce. We also suspect that imperfect information is generating statistical discrimination against classes of workers, particularly women part-timers. Perhaps the longitudinal information brought out in this book can help to improve the perception of a generation's human resources.

Though unequal treatment may be a continuing fact, these indications of the mechanisms that sustain it suggest that it is not an immutable fact of life. Our estimates of the extent of unequal treatment in the post–Equal Pay Act era suggest sluggish progress, if anything. Does this mean that equal pay policy is now mature? Has it gone about as far as it can go, or is there more to be done?

Policy Implications

Whether muscle power or patriarchal power was the reason for paying men more than women historically, these reasons no longer justify unequal pay. Modern statutes have ordained that men and women should be paid the same for work of equal value. But men in contemporary Britain are still paid nearly £1.50 per hour for every £1 paid to the average woman worker (all ages in 1990, allowing for nearly half the women employees being part-timers). There is perhaps inequality in access to the chance to accumulate earning assets, and in access to the more remunerative parts of the labor market. Yet there also remains some unequal treatment for equal human capital characteristics, as shown by our study of the cohorts. Should we conclude that equal pay has only partially succeeded, and that the inherent limitations of the legislation, noted in chapter 1, would lead one to expect such imperfection?

Laws about equal pay do not operate in a vacuum. They are better backed up by antidiscrimination machinery promoting equal opportunity in employment, and opportunities to combine employment and parental responsibilities. But the key to effective implementation seems to be the set of institutions that centralize the wage-setting process. In a labor market that is highly regulated in other respects, the implementation of equal pay has been more rapid and closer to completion.

British equal pay law came in at a time when the wage-setting process was dominated by national agreements and regulated by incomes policies (Fallick and Elliot 1981). Wages councils set the minimum wages in the lowest-paid industries, where many workers were women. During the course of the 1980s, the Thatcher government embarked on a program of deregulating and decentralizing the labor market. The powers of unions were reduced, the coverage of collective bargaining declined, and wages councils were weakened and then abolished. The structure of the labor market was affected by privatization, subcontracting, and casualization. Some of these developments—for example, the weakening of union power—may have brought men's wages closer to women's by reducing what were effectively discriminatory structures. Other developments, particularly the abolition of wages councils and the proliferation of part-time contracts, are likely to have intensified the economic disadvantages of women doing part-time work (Hunter and Rimmer 1995).

Possible measures to strengthen the equal pay law include improved resourcing and training of tribunals, more resources for the Equal Opportunities Commission, legal aid for claimants, the introduction of class action suits, the shift of the burden of proof to the employer, simplification of procedures, and the enshrining of equal status for part-timers in job contracts. Although the Equal Opportunities Commission recommended such measures to the government regularly during the 1990s, there has been no official response. Furthermore, the advent of deregulation makes it unlikely that any such steps would have quick or widespread effect—the old transmission mechanisms have gone. For the writ of equal pay to reach the lowest-paid women, in part-time, women-only casual employment, the tribunal-based approach would have to be strengthened almost beyond credibility. Women would need to have the right, the resources, and the confidence to make a case against one employer based on a comparator in another employment. The reconstitution of some sort of minimum wage seems a more promising way forward.

A minimum wage is the main plank of a raft of policies to improve the terms of part-time employment proposed by Gill (1995). The establishment of part-timers' rights would be affected by the adoption of the EC draft directive on part-time and fixed-term workers, and by the effective abolition of the lower earnings limit to national insurance coverage.

There is, of course, a concern that policies which raise wages may backfire on the groups they are intended to help, if it leads to their being "priced out of the market." In general, the pay increases at the time the Equal Pay Act was introduced did not have such an adverse effect on employment. Manning (1996) has suggested that the monopsonistic structure of labor markets for British women could account for the phenomenon. This implies that raising the rate of pay would reduce exploitation but not employment. The evidence we have found is consistent with the idea that women—especially if working part-time—with a low range of spatial mobility and domestic time constraints take jobs where the employer can set the wage. The market failure, which results from the existence of monopsonistic power, justifies government intervention. Interventions to correct the market failure might be minimum wages (Machin and Manning 1992), equal rates for full-time and part-time workers, measures designed to increase job mobility (child care, public transport, training), or, probably better still, a combination. Our finding applies particularly to part-timers who should therefore stand to make genuine gains from interventions on their behalf.

Nevertheless, simply raising low pay is not enough for women, their families, and the economy as a whole to reap the gains from opening up equal opportunities (Humphries and Rubery 1995). As the Equal Opportunities Commission (1995) stresses, the gains are in efficiency not just equity: " ... a wide range of measures to remove obstacles to equality of opportunity ... should unlock the skills, talents and creativity which are still too often fettered and constrained by traditional attitudes and stereotypes about the roles of both men and women." Such measures should probably start in the home, in the gendered upbringing children receive. The commission's policy initiatives start in schools with widening the choice of subjects available to girls and boys, as well as addressing the problem of male underachievement.

Another area in which our evidence endorses the need for action is in job training for women. Training programs hitherto tended to reproduce occupational sex-stereotyping, where they reach women at all (Felstead 1995). They need to be implemented with more "gender awareness" and an effort to offer women training in nontraditional areas. Training programs also need to be more flexible with respect to women's domestic demands. Courses are often held at times women cannot be free, and seldom come with services or cash for child care (though there have been exceptions for single mothers). The general lack of access to training for women, especially part-timers, as highlighted in chapter 5, contributes to the vertical segregation we detected, and to the low-skill, low-productivity equilibrium identified by Bruegel and Perrons (1995).

Policies are also still needed to facilitate combining employment and family life. The consolidation of maternity leave law is on the agenda, but a high priority should also be given to recognizing fathers' rights to time off work, both in the form of paternity leave at the time of the birth and parental leave at later stages. There is also a long way to go before good-quality, reliable child care is accessible and affordable by all. A climate of genuine choice about the sharing of roles, and about the ways parenthood and paid work may be combined, would offer more alternative models to the next generation. It is more likely to flourish in a climate where equal pay and equal opportunities are taken seriously. As Dex and Sewell (1995) argue, the indirect effect of such machinery in putting "gender on the agenda" is as important as what may be a rather limited direct impact. Indeed, the Equal Opportunities Commission (1996) sees their first task as "mainstreaming" gender—raising general awareness of sex equality and building it into everyday life.

This book should inform this debate. We have shown how the gains from equal pay and equal opportunities legislation have been greatest for an elite of well-educated women. As unequal treatment of men and women abates, inequalities between women (and between men) have increased. The less well paid women are trapped in the vicious circle of the low skilled. Some women, as Hakim (1996) suggests, many have chosen to concentrate on being wives and mothers. Such choices should not be labeled "failures." The evidence of this study is that such choices are still constrained and distorted, by the prevalence of unequal pay. This imports inefficiency as well as inequity into the gender order. Can the knowledge-based economy afford not to mobilize women's brainpower?

The increasingly knowledge-based economy, still needs paid and unpaid time to be devoted to caring activities. There is a danger that such work will continue to be undervalued and delegated to women, particularly the unskilled. Folbre (1994) calls for a fundamental rethinking of the values leading industrial societies toward the unviability of social reproduction. She calls for a gender-neutral family policy, of which equal treatment of men and women in the labor market is only one part. The level playing field cannot extend to all parts of the labor market unless it also extends to the home.

Appendixes

3.1 Variable Definitions

Table A3.1 provides a definition of the variables included in the general specification of the equations estimated in the following chapters.

Earnings are defined as gross hourly wages and, due to data limitations, they include overtime payments. The definition of part-timers is, whenever possible, self-declared. In the case of NCDS this information, however, has been supplemented by the details of the number of hours worked for those members who had not provided the self-assessed definition.

The first three subsets of variables entering the earnings equations are "pure human capital" endowments, and we expect them to have a positive effect on wages. They are included (at times with slight variations) in the specification of the earnings equations in all chapters. The rationale for dividing work experience into two periods is the hypothesis that recent work experience has a stronger effect on wages than earlier experience. The break at age 26 reflects one of the points at which data was collected for the 1946 cohort, and it shifts to 23 in chapter 5, when the analysis is limited to NCDS. The most recent sweep of the MRC available to us was carried out around January 1978, just before the respondents' 32nd birthday, and that of the NCDS was conducted from the April following the respondents' 33rd birthday. The time covered by recent work experience for the MRC could be as much as twenty-four months less than NCDS. We do not specify any quadratic terms in experience, as we do not observe enough years in the labor force to expect returns to start diminishing, as they might over twenty or thirty years.

The regional dummy reflects differences in labor-market condition and living costs between the Southeast and the rest of the country. Given the relatively large number of missing values for this variable, we have

Table A3.1
Variable definitions

Dependent variable	
Log hourly wage	Gross wage per hour worked (including overtime)
Explanatory variables	
Personal	
Ability at 11	General ability as measured at age 11
O-levels	Dummy = 1 if highest educational qualification level = O-level
A-levels	Dummy = 1 if highest educational qualification = A-level
Diploma	Dummy = 1 if highest qualification = diploma from nondegree higher education
Degree	Dummy = 1 if highest qualification = university degree (reference category = no qualifications)
Training	Dummy = 1 if ever had training in current job
Work experience, 23–33	Years in paid employment since age 23
Service	Years of service with current employer
Southeast	Dummy = 1 if interviewed in Southeast, 1991[a]
Employer	
Small firm	Dummy = 1 if firm employs less than 25
Large firm	Dummy = 1 if firm employs more than 100 (reference category = firm has 25–100 employees)
Private sector	Dummy = 1 if firm privately owned, rather than public or non-profit
Business	Dummy = 1 if industry = business services incl. real estate, renting, research, and business activities
Catering	Dummy = 1, if industry = hotels and restaurants
Miscellaneous services	Dummy = 1 if industry = community and personal services other than health, social work, education, and domestic service; includes sport and recreation
Education	Dummy = 1, if industry = schools and higher education
Finance	Dummy = 1, if industry = banking or financial services
Publishing	Dummy = 1, if industry = printing and publishing
Textile and leather	Dummy = 1, if industry = textiles and leather manufacturing
Transport	Dummy = 1, if industry = transport services
Machine and equipment	Dummy = 1, if industry = manufacture of machines and equipment (reference category = other industries)
Job	
Employer paid for training	Dummy = 1 if current employer ever provided or financed training
Hours flexible	Dummy = 1 if employee reports a choice about hours worked
Supervision	Dummy = 1 if has supervisory responsibility for other employees
Travel-to-work	Journey to work time measured in minutes
Union member	Dummy = 1 if employee a union member

Table A3.1 (continued)

Company car	Dummy = 1 if employer provides a car
Medical insurance	Dummy = 1 if covered by medical insurance provided by employer
Pension	Dummy = 1 if covered by employer pension scheme
Occupation	
Professionals	Dummy = 1 if job in RG Class 1
Teachers	Dummy = 1 if job = teacher (not university)
Nurses	Dummy = 1 if job in nursing or paramedic or social work
Other intermediate	Dummy = 1 if job other intermediate nonmanual
Clerical	Dummy = 1 if job secretary, clerk, etc.
Service and shop	Dummy = 1 if job routine service or retail, e.g., bar attendant, shop assistant
Skilled ocupations	Dummy = 1 if job skilled manual, e.g., cook, painter, train driver (reference category = semiskilled and unskilled, e.g., cleaner, laborer)
Feminized	Dummy = 1 if occupational unit group (1990 classification) more than 50% females in 1991 census, workers of all ages, Great Britain

Note: a. Given their large number, we have included the missing cases of the "region of the interview" variable in the zero category, having tested that they are not statistically different from the other cases in this category.

included these cases in the "zero" category. We have then tested for any bias resulting from this procedure by including a missing-region flag variable. The low *t*-ratio on the coefficient of this variable allows us to drop the dummy without the risk of bias to the result. Chapter 5 also includes a number of variables reflecting employer and job characteristics. The details of these variables and the rationale for their inclusion is given in chapter 5. Their definition is included in table A3.1. Similarly, the variables included in the selection equations differ across chapters and their details are described in the relevant chapter, although their definition is included in table A3.1.

3.2   Data Cleaning

Two major cleaning exercises were carried out on NCDS5, with numerous and thorough checks of the data. One concerns the wages of employees. Among cases where wages appeared to be reported, we looked for four types of problem: (1) inconsistency between net and gross earning values (112 cases); (2) suspiciously low wages (only one report of less than £0.50 an hour); (3) suspiciously high wages (six workers appear to earn more than £50.00 an hour); (4) questionably high hours (1,159 workers reported working fifty hours a week or more). We dealt with the first of these problems in a variety of ways that have allowed us to "rescue" 97 of the 112 cases. The amendments were divided into two categories: definite and probable changes, with a flag variable marking the probable changes. The sole worker with an hourly wage lower than £0.50 was dropped. Flag variables were also defined for others with surprisingly high wages or hours. However, tests on these flags did not suggest any significant difference between workers with suspicious data and the rest. In all 6,800 employees with valid wage data were accepted as suitable cases for analysis. Reporting a long working week is actually not unusual for British men (Ward et al. 1993).

The second cleaning operation concerned the NCDS5 job histories, which were not subject to much checking before delivery. Concurrent spells in more than one job (or in more than one employment status) had been reconciled as far as possible. Unaccounted parts of the job history have been assigned, also as far as possible, to the appropriate employment status. In cases where twelve or fewer months were unassignable, unaccounted time was assumed to be without employment. If more than twelve months were missing and not reasonably assignable, the cases were rejected. In sum, we succeeded in reconstructing full employment histories from age 18 for 74% of the NCDS cohort members and full histories from age 23 for 85%.

The project was also among the first to make use of the recoded occupations for the cohort members' current or most recent job. The recoding was done in SSRU over the summer of 1994. This was done after it became apparent that there was an unacceptably high level of error, at least in the detail, of occupations coded by the original automated process. Other occupations in NCDS5 were being checked after the end of this project, and no use is made of them here. Data on industry was not originally coded at all. It was added to the data set in time to be incorporated in the analyses reported in chapter 5.

4   The Selection Equation

As explained more extensively in chapter 2, the problem of potential selection bias in the estimation of earnings equations for women arises from the fact that wages can only be observed for those women who are currently working. If there are systematic unobservable differences between the women in a job and the others, confining the analysis to current employees may give a biased representation of the full set of wage opportunities available to them. Heckman's (1979) answer to the issue of selectivity derives from the basic participation criterion, according to which a woman would decide to take a job if the wage offered exceeds her shadow wage at home, w^H, where

$$\ln w^H = \delta Z + e^H; \tag{A4.1}$$

e^H is an error term, δ is a vector of coefficients, and Z is a vector of personal characteristics determining productivity at home. These include all the characteristics of relevance to the labor market, X, plus others. The subscript i, for individual women, is omitted.

Thus a woman's propensity to participate in the labor market can be proxied by a continuous variable, y^*, defined as

$$y^* = \ln w - \ln w^H = \beta X - \delta Z + (e - e^H). \tag{A4.2}$$

In the simple formulation there are only two possible employment conditions, in-paid-work and not-in-paid-work. When the value of y^* is positive, the woman decides to take paid work. Consequently, the expected log value of a woman's earnings is dependent not only on her labor-market characteristics, X, but is defined as

$$E(\ln w) = \beta X + E(e|y^* > 0), \tag{A4.3}$$

where the second term is the "sample selection rule" that corrects the market wage to account for the woman's propensity to be in employment.

The sample selection rule is the product of a scalar, σ, constant for all the selected cases, and λ, a term that varies across individuals. The former is a function of the standard deviation of the error terms in the earnings equation and in the shadow "home wage" equation (A4.1), and their correlation. The woman-specific term, λ, reflects the woman's predicted probability of participation, given other known characteristics. λ is defined as the inverse of the Mills ratio, the ratio of the ordinate of the standard normal density divided by the standard normal distribution, both evaluated at (y^*).

λ is calculated from a regression of a woman's employment status upon her personal characteristics (i.e., the participation equation). So far we treat participation as one status compared with one alternative, nonparticipation, as does much of the literature. The dependent variable in this case is a binary discrete variable that takes the value of 1 if a woman is in the labor market, and a value of 0 otherwise. The model can be specified as a bivariate probit or logit, and either yields an estimate of λ. This is then included in the earnings equation (A4.3) to correct for selectivity into employment. Its coefficient is a parameter σ, which could have either a positive or negative sign depending on whether the otherwise unmeasured peculiarities of participants compared with nonparticipants lead to higher or lower wages. The resulting earnings equation is therefore given by

$$\ln w = \beta X + \sigma \lambda + \varepsilon. \tag{A4.4}$$

It is possible to allow for more than one type of outcome (i.e., full-time and part-time). The selection equation can take the form of an ordered (or multinomial) probit or logit. The participation equation would then estimate for each individual woman the probabilities of her being in each of the possible forms of paid work. The status-specific earnings equation would include the different λ's associated with full- and part-time work.

In this chapter we allow for three possible employment conditions: not-in-paid-work, working part-time, and working full-time. This is a multinomial choice variable that is inherently ordered. We therefore adopt an ordered probit model (Greene 1992). Since we also wish to test for differences between the two cohorts, our participation equation takes the form

$$y^* = \chi \cdot dum + \delta \cdot Z + \phi \cdot [Z \cdot dum] + v, \tag{A4.5}$$

where y^*, δ and Z have the meaning described above, dum is a dummy variable taking the value 1 for an observation in NCDS, χ is its coefficient, ϕ is the coefficient vector on the interaction terms, and v is a standard normal variate. The participation criterion is as follows.

$0 > y^* \Rightarrow y = 0$ and the woman does not work,

$0 < y^* < \mu \Rightarrow y = 1$ and the woman works part-time,

$\mu < y^* \Rightarrow y = 2$ and the woman works full-time.

The μ's is an unknown parameter indicating the threshold between part-time and full-time work. Its significance in our participation equations suggests a well-defined threshold between part-time and full-time employment in both cohorts, and generates distinct probabilities for the two sorts of participation, and hence separate χ's for each type of employment.

Table A4.1 gives a detailed definition of the variables entering the participation equation for the two cohorts. The pooled sample size for this specification across cohorts is 4,146. Women employees without valid information on wages are included in the "nonparticipant" category. Our estimates begin with a general specification of the ordered probit, and we use likelihood ratio tests to search for a parsimonious specification. All

Table A4.1
Ordered probit: Variable definitions

Categories	
Not working	Not valid wage reported
Part-timer	Self-declared part-timers or—if this missing—number of hours worked <30
Full-timer	Self-declared full-timers or—if this missing—number of hours worked >30

Explanatory variables

Personal characteristics

Ability at 11	General ability as measured at age 11
O-levels	Dummy = 1 if highest educational qualification O-level
Work experience, 26–32	Recent work experience (in years)

Partner left education

<17	Dummy = 1 if spouse left education before 17th birthday
17–18	Dummy = 1 if spouse left education between 17th and 19th birthday
19+	Dummy = 1 if spouse left education after 19th birthday

Income/wealth

Nonworking income	Value of nonworking income, including nonincome-related benefit (£100)
House tenure	Dummy = 1 if household owns house

Family commitments

Ever married	Dummy = 1 if married, separated, divorced, or widowed
Youngest child <5	Dummy = 1 if youngest child <5
Youngest child 6–11	Dummy = 1 if youngest child 6–11
Youngest child 12–16	Dummy = 1 if youngest child 12–16

variables with t ratios less than 1.64 (significant at 10% level) are then dropped and the model reestimated. Seven variables were excluded: number of children, missing value for general ability score, highest qualification A-level, highest qualification teaching, highest qualification degree, tenant of Local Authorities or Housing Associations, and renting from the private sector.

6   Investigating Selection Bias and Endogeneity of Motherhood

The full multinomial model is specified as:

$$S^* = \gamma \mathbf{Z} + u \tag{A6.1}$$

$$w_k = \beta_k \mathbf{X}_k + e_k, \tag{A6.2}$$

where S^* is an unobservable variable that determines the woman's motherhood/employment status, Z is a vector of variables affecting the probability of individual women belonging to any of the six categories, w is the log of hourly wages, k identifies the relevant motherhood/employment category, X stands for a vector of variables affecting wages, u and e are error terms, and the superscript i for the individual has been omitted for simplicity. S^* is proxied by a sixfold indicator variable defined as

$$S^* = \begin{cases} \text{(i) if childless and not employed,} \\ \text{(ii) if childless and employed part-time,} \\ \text{(iii) if childless and employed full-time,} \\ \text{(iv) if mother and not employed,} \\ \text{(v) if mother and employed part-time,} \\ \text{(vi) if mother and employed full-time.} \end{cases} \qquad (A6.3)$$

The status-specific wage equations are then estimated as

$$w_k = \beta X_k + \eta \lambda_k + \varepsilon_k, \qquad (A6.4)$$

where λ_k is the status-specific selection term defined as in appendix 4.

A list of the explanatory variables included is given in table A6.1. The results of the estimation of selection equations into six possible states for the two cohorts are given in table A6.2. They appear to fit the data better for NCDS than for MRC. Where significant, as expected, (1) the probability of being a full-time worker increases with education and ability and declines with nonlabor income and with the level of education of the partner, (2) the probability of being a mother declines with the partner's level of education and is higher in the Southeast.

As in chapter 4 we find that that the association of home ownership with the probability of employment has opposite and significant signs for the two cohorts. This may reflect the fact that women in the later cohort may be more likely to be working to pay off the mortgage, while home ownership in the earlier cohort may have been more closely associated with higher socioeconomic status and higher wealth and thus with lower likelihood of employment. Within the 1958 cohort the probability of being a childless woman increases with the age when the cohort member's mother had her first child and is higher for girls who said they intended to remain childless.

The presence of selection bias is tested by reference to the coefficient of the λ_k term in the earnings equation. The model is identified by the omission of work experience and job tenure from the participation equation.

Table A6.1
Multinomial logit: Variable definitions

Multinomial categories	
Not-in-labor-force	No valid wage reported
Part-timer	Self-declared part-time employees or—if this missing—number of hours worked <30
Full-timer	Self-declared full-time employees or—if this missing—number of hours worked >30
Mother	If number of living-in children >0
Maternity leaver	If returned to paid work within twelve months of first birth
Nonmother	No children in the household at 32/3
Explanatory variables	
Personal characteristics	
Ability at 11	General ability as measured at age 11
O-levels	Dummy = 1 if highest educational qualification O-level
A-levels	Dummy = 1 if highest educational qualification A-level
Diploma	Dummy = 1 if highest educational qualification FE diploma
Degree	Dummy = 1 if highest educational qualification university degree
Social background	
Father social class 1 or 2	Dummy = 1 if father social class is 1 or 2 when cohort member was 15/16
Partner's education	
O-levels and A-levels	Dummy = 1 if spouse's highest level of education = O- or A-levels (NCDS only)
Further/higher education	Dummy = 1 if spouse's highest level of education > A-level
Age	Partner's age in years (MRC only)
Income/wealth	
Nonworking income	Value of nonworking income, including partner's earnings and nonincome-related benefits
House tenure	Dummy = 1 if household owns house
Attitudes at 16	
No wish to have children	Dummy = 1 if desired number of children = 0 (NCDS only)
Expects to be late parent	Dummy = 1 if desired age of motherhood >25 (NCDS only)
High ambition	Dummy = 1 if cohort member declares to be ambitious (MRC only)
Maternal characteristics	
Age at motherhood	Cohort member's mother's age at motherhood
Others	
Southeast 1974	Dummy = 1 if resident in the Southeast at 16 (in 1974) (NCDS only)

Table A6.2
Multinomial logit equation with six categories of employment and motherhood status (MRC and NCDS cohorts)

MRC	All women (n = 771)									
	Mothers				Childless					
	Part-time (n = 281)		Full-time (n = 123)		Nonworking (n = 43)		Part-time (n = 32)		Full-time (n = 150)	
Variables	Coefficient	t-values	Coefficient	t-values	Coefficient	t-values	Coefficient	t-values	Coefficient	t-values
Constant	1.943	1.59	3.775	2.84	3.873	2.35	0.675	0.31	2.887	2.03
Woman's education										
Ability at 11	−0.004	0.32	−0.006	0.47	−0.006	0.49	0.001	0.02	−0.004	0.22
O-levels	0.084	0.30	0.361	1.07	0.785	1.70	0.070	0.12	1.348	3.59
A-Levels	−0.391	0.94	0.338	0.72	−0.310	0.40	−0.483	0.57	0.165	0.30
Diploma	−1.276	2.11	0.775	1.33	0.694	0.85	−1.797	1.06	1.025	1.67
Degree	−1.310	1.69	−0.553	0.57	0.026	0.02	−0.090	0.08	1.273	1.75
Social background										
Father social class 1 or 2	−0.330	1.04	−0.459	1.13	0.054	0.10	−0.013	0.02	−0.612	1.50
Partner's characteristics										
Further and higher education	1.413	1.43	−0.618	0.44	0.113	0.06	−8.509	0.06	−0.440	0.31
Age	0.016	0.54	−0.078	2.52	−0.085	2.50	−0.085	2.04	−0.113	3.61
Income/wealth										
Nonworking income	−0.002	0.27	0.012	1.11	−0.044	2.43	0.004	0.25	−0.038	2.99
House tenure	−0.468	2.05	−1.106	3.96	−0.616	1.44	−0.519	1.14	−1.171	3.61
Attitudes at 16										
High ambition	0.064	0.23	−0.321	0.93	−0.169	0.34	0.320	0.59	0.622	1.79
Woman's own mother										
Age at motherhood	−0.043	1.38	−0.057	1.51	−0.058	1.02	0.009	0.15	0.042	1.08

NCDS	All women (n = 2,782)									
	Mothers				Childless					
	Part-time (n = 750)		Full-time (n = 470)		Nonworking (n = 156)		Part-time (n = 43)		Full-time (n = 631)	
Variables	Coefficient	t-values	Coefficient	t-values	Coefficient	t-values	Coefficient	t-values	Coefficient	t-values
Constant	−0.277	0.82	−0.448	1.16	−2.052	3.70	−2.842	2.95	−1.605	4.22
Woman's education										
Ability at 11	−0.000	0.07	0.000	0.18	0.004	0.80	−0.002	0.45	0.013	2.93
O-levels	0.065	0.53	0.379	2.50	0.166	0.65	0.067	1.69	0.056	3.47
A-Levels	−0.190	0.86	0.558	2.34	0.367	0.97	−0.086	0.11	0.999	4.30
Diploma	0.472	2.60	1.201	6.03	0.994	3.22	0.842	1.53	1.341	6.43
Degree	0.192	0.74	1.317	4.97	1.495	4.22	1.223	1.85	1.822	7.04
Social background										
Father social class 1 or 2	−0.121	0.85	−0.068	0.43	0.395	1.82	0.444	1.16	−0.125	0.83
Partner's education										
O-levels and A-levels	0.353	2.06	−0.189	1.05	−1.976	8.35	−0.529	1.22	−1.790	10.65
Further and higher	−0.095	0.40	−0.605	2.39	−1.986	6.06	−0.930	1.35	−2.099	8.68
Income/wealth										
Nonworking income	−0.022	1.44	−0.079	0.52	0.010	0.43	−0.115	0.96	−0.099	3.01
House tenure	0.396	3.07	0.487	3.17	0.027	0.12	−0.342	0.94	0.715	4.71
Attitudes at 16										
No wish to have children	0.690	1.76	−0.159	0.29	1.389	3.01	0.755	0.90	0.443	1.07
Expects to be late parent	−0.229	1.57	−0.309	1.86	0.221	0.98	0.351	0.91	−0.008	0.05
Woman's own mother										
Age at motherhood	−0.009	0.69	−0.002	1.33	0.045	2.05	0.009	0.24	0.048	3.34
Others										
Southeast in 1974	−0.016	0.13	−0.236	1.64	−0.188	0.88	−0.302	0.77	−0.014	0.11

Table A6.3
Multinomial logit equation with nine categories of employment, motherhood, and maternity leave status (NCDS cohort)

Variables	All women (n = 2,546)										Childless women					
	Non–maternity leavers				Maternity leavers											
	Part-time (n = 413)		Full-time (n = 150)		Non-working (n = 204)		Part-time (n = 242)		Full-time (n = 270)		Non-working (n = 156)		Part-time (n = 43)		Full-time (n = 631)	
	Coef.	t-val.	Coef.	t-val.	Coef.	t-val.	Coef.	t-val.	Coef.	t-val.	Coef.	t-val.	Coef.	t-val.	Coef.	t-val.
Constant	−0.017	0.04	−0.962	1.50	−1.746	2.95	−2.700	4.56	−1.495	2.69	−1.702	2.76	−2.222	2.14	−1.345	3.06
Woman's education																
Ability at 11	0.002	0.44	0.011	1.39	0.006	0.78	0.003	0.41	0.008	1.24	0.004	0.51	−0.008	0.61	0.014	2.53
O-levels	0.181	1.10	0.361	1.55	0.477	2.17	0.281	1.33	0.570	2.62	0.319	1.18	0.938	2.21	0.723	4.07
A-Levels	−0.052	0.18	0.146	0.36	0.209	0.58	−0.009	0.02	0.817	2.56	0.476	1.18	0.149	0.18	1.124	4.27
Diploma	0.432	1.65	1.123	3.46	0.911	2.94	1.377	4.96	1.697	6.09	1.284	3.77	1.251	2.14	1.633	6.60
Degree	−0.032	0.07	0.788	1.33	1.571	3.78	1.787	4.45	2.281	5.86	2.180	5.03	2.116	2.86	2.504	7.22
Social background																
Father social class 1 or 2	−0.427	2.12	−0.418	1.48	−0.075	0.34	0.112	0.55	0.044	0.22	0.337	1.44	0.421	1.07	−0.185	1.06
Partner's education																
O-levels and A-levels	0.194	0.90	−0.361	1.35	0.103	0.36	0.875	2.70	−0.153	0.61	−1.976	7.80	−0.512	1.14	−1.772	9.21
Further and higher	−0.125	0.39	−1.413	2.89	0.242	0.66	0.381	0.95	−0.431	1.30	−1.939	5.40	−0.853	1.20	−2.041	7.15
Income/wealth																
Nonworking income	−0.000	0.47	−0.000	0.24	0.000	0.08	−0.000	0.90	−0.000	0.20	0.000	0.54	−0.001	0.92	−0.001	2.69
House tenure	0.399	2.40	0.236	1.04	0.493	2.22	0.730	3.30	0.825	3.79	0.126	0.95	−0.206	0.55	0.822	4.87

Attitudes at 16															
No wish to have children	0.899	1.35	0.762	1.03	−0.131	0.18	−0.746	0.91	−0.871	1.06	1.271	2.46	0.680	0.79	0.293	0.61
Expects to be late parent	−0.357	1.79	−0.759	2.39	−0.174	0.75	−0.087	0.40	−0.143	0.68	0.230	0.95	0.343	0.87	−0.011	0.06
Maternal characteristics																
Age at motherhood	−0.022	1.19	−0.018	0.71	0.103	0.14	0.013	0.62	−0.021	1.01	0.043	1.83	0.010	0.25	0.047	2.81
Others																
Southeast in 1974	−0.163	1.00	0.487	1.72	−0.183	0.91	0.105	0.57	−0.170	0.92	−0.238	1.05	−0.349	0.88	−0.075	0.49

The latter also includes a number of variables not entering the earnings equation. In the more general model we find the selection term is significant only for MRC childless women who work full-time.

The analysis is then extended to allow for structural differences between those mothers who have continuous employment history ("maternity leavers") and those who left the labor market around childbearing. Once again the problem of endogeneity of the decision of whether or not to maintain continuous employment is dealt with by means of a multinomial logit. The new specification allows for the simultaneous determination of maternal status, current employment status, and employment status at childbirth so that S^* is a ninefold categorical variable. For each cohort six status-specific wage equations are estimated allowing for selectivity bias.

Table A6.2 presents the results of the nine-category multinomial logit. The results are not dissimilar from those in table A6.1. Few individual parameters are well determined, but those for higher qualifications are particularly strong for maternity leavers, most of all for full-time employment. It is interesting to note that not all mothers who had continuity in employment at the time of the first birth were to be found in full-time employment in 1991: 270 were employed full-time, 242 part-time, and 204 were out of the labor market. Joshi et al. (1996) found that having continuity at the first maternity raised participation propensities but not to the extent that it precluded subsequent withdrawals.

Family formation behavior was clearly related to measured socioeconomic factors (and the propensity to stay in the labor market on childbearing for the later cohort). The tests we have carried out suggest that the women who delayed or avoided motherhood were not systematically different on unmeasured characteristics after allowing for the effects of variables we have measured. Controlling for factors measured from childhood onward is an unusual opportunity, thanks to the cohort studies.

Notes

Chapter 1

1. The unemployed are not included in figure 1.1 though they are in the labor force, as presented in table 1.1. The sources for figure 1.1 are the Census of Employment and National Insurance statistics, adapted from Bartley et al. 1997 in Charlton and Murphy 1997, figure 6.19, with authors' estimate of women's part-time employment in 1961 (Joshi and Owen 1987).

2. Mincer and Polacek (1974), Becker (1981, 1985), and Hakim (1991, 1996) favor the view that there is at least some causality from domestic orientation to low wages.

3. Gronau (1988) tests a model in which wages, planned separations, on-the-job training, and skill intensity of the job are jointly determined. The last factor is not well explained by traditional sex-role differences.

4. See Cigno (1991) and Becker (1985), though the latter admits that the division of labor need not be along sex lines. See Joshi (1998) for further discussion.

5. De Cooman et al. (1987) show a link between the rapid change in relative wages in the mid-1970s and the postponement of the first birth in England and Wales. See also Olsen (1994), for a review of fertility and the female labor market in the United States.

6. A related argument was used in Sweden at the beginning of the century. Women knew how to cook, wash, and sew, and hence did not need to be paid as much as men (Löfström 1996).

7. Full-time employees with at least two years' service, or part-timers with five or more years.

8. *R v Secretary of State for Employment ex parte Seymour Smith (1995)*, referred to the European Court of Justice by the House of Lords in 1997.

9. The evidence from Sweden on this comes from personal communication from several Swedish economists: Eskil Wadensjo, Siv Gustafsson, and Åsa Löfström. Our difficulty in finding a published citation could reflect an instance of publication bias against negative findings.

10. Oaxaca's D_f and D_m convert differences in logarithms into differentials as a percentage of the lower-paid group's average. See equations (2.3) and (2.4).

11. The median hourly earnings of full-time adult employees is equivalent to the geometric mean of the cohorts' wages analyzed in the regressions on the assumption that the distribution of earnings is approximately lognormal.

12. The Family Expenditure Survey also suggests that the gap between the wages of women in part-time and full-time jobs did not open up until the second half of the 1970s (Harkness 1996). The improved position for full-timers was offset by deterioration for part-timers.

Chapter 2

1. The classification of discrimination that follows is based on Bosworth et al. 1996.

2. The latter option is available only to the monopsonistic employer who faces an upward-sloping supply curve from women. If the supply curve of both groups is perfectly elastic—that is, the labor market is competitive—the employer's taste for discrimination results in men being paid more than the competitive wage.

3. It is worth noting that this specification of the earnings function assumes the wage rate to have a lognormal distribution, i.e., the log of the wage to be normally distributed, with mean zero and variance σ_S^2. In this case $m_S = \exp(\beta_S \bar{X})$ estimates the median, rather than the mean wage rate for sex S. To estimate the mean, we would need to use $\bar{w}_S = \exp(\beta_S \bar{X}) + 0.5\sigma_S^2$. In general $0.5\sigma_S^2$ is very small and the adjustment is usually neglected, as here.

4. This formula expressed the index as the geometric mean of wages. If the index is to be expressed as the arithmetic mean of wages, the formula would be:

$$D_f = \{\exp[(\beta_m - \beta_f) \cdot \bar{X}_f) - 0.5(\sigma_f^2 - \sigma_m^2)] - 1\} \cdot 100.$$

5. See, for example, Gunderson 1989.

Chapter 3

1. Those with fathers in the urban working class are given a weight four times greater than the other cases.

2. Enquiries about the MRC data and its documentation should be addressed to the MRC National Survey Director at University College London.

3. For further details of these studies, see Shepherd 1993, Fogelman 1983, Fogelman and Wedge 1981, Ferri 1993, Ekinsmyth et al. 1992, Butler and Bonham 1963, and Butler and Golding 1986.

4. This also includes an account of the preschool facilities used by the MRC cohort as children themselves. These were largely nursery schools, if anything.

5. The process continued, the participation rate for the 1970 cohort in 1996 was 78%, 65% full-time (Joshi and Paci 1997), which accords with figure 3.2.

6. The occupational histories of NCDS have not been fully analyzed.

7. We did not attempt to incorporate wage data from earlier sweeps. For the MRC study, the numbers of women observed with wages at both ages 26 and 32 would be too small to analyze full-timers and part-timers separately. Joshi and Newell (1989) had 242 women in their two-wage sample. We did not use NCDS data for age 23 because this would have required another major data-cleaning exercise. This reconciliation of employment histories across the two sweeps has now been done, under the direction of Peter Dolton, but was not ready for use here.

8. "Dimensions of Health over Persons, Time, and Place." H. Joshi, R. Wiggins, M. Bartley, and P. Paci, funded by ESRC.

Chapter 4

1. The equations in (3.2) are estimated using LIMDEP (Greene 1992), a package that yields the correct estimates of the parameter standard errors.

2. Whether region of residence is inside or outside the Southeast was proxied by the regional base of the interviewer in NCDS.

3. A difference between the specification of the earnings equations in this chapter and those used in the rest of the book is the inclusion of a dummy variable for cases with a missing score on general ability. The variable has a relatively large number of missing values. To avoid losing these observations, we have imputed to these cases the mean value of general ability for their employment category. We have then included one indicator variable denoting missing ability to flag the cases concerned. Having gained the insight that those with missing information (and who subsequently remained in contact with the survey) were not systematically different from other cohort members, we felt justified in dropping this variable from the equation.

4. The interaction term between early experience and high educational qualification is intended as a crude adjustment for the hypothesis that early work experience is less important for late school leavers than for other workers.

5. Given the interest in the selection model, in the comparison among women we retained the sample selection term for the test of stability across cohorts, although its coefficient is not significantly different from zero. When considering gender differences among full-timers, however, the selection term is omitted from the women's equation to make the comparison between the coefficients of the two groups easier. The two sets of results for women full-timers are virtually identical.

6. This could reflect the growing polarization of labor force attachment associated with early and late childbearing explored in further length by Macran et al. (1996), Dex et al. (1996), and Joshi et al. (1996)

7. In this table, differences associated with the selection terms are treated as any other parameter or attribute differences, that is, we concentrate on the wage gap conditional on participation, not on wage offers also facing nonparticipants. The difference is the product of the mean lambda for each employment status and its parameter. It measures the market value of any net differences in unspecified characteristics that set the participants apart. It amounts to one or two percentage points, in either direction, in the discrimination index. The practice of keeping this term in the decomposition was adopted by Dolton and Makepeace (1986). It contrasts with that of Ermisch and Wright (1992 and 1993) and Wright and Ermisch (1991), who adjust the wage gap for selection effects before undertaking further decomposition of the resulting gap in estimated 'wage offers', rather than actual wages.

8. It is to be noted that the value of the mean discrimination term emerging from table 3.6 is not the same as the parameter gap at the means of the $X's$. This is due to the fact that one is the product of means while the other is the mean of a product. The two are obviously not identical.

Chapter 5

1. The hypothesis of selectivity bias among women was tested using the ordered-probit Heckman procedure described in the appendix to chapter 4. The coefficient of the lambda term in the earnings equation of both part-time and full-time women was consistently insignificant, leading us to reject the possibility of selection bias among those observed with wages. The estimates for the selection-adjusted models are therefore not reported.

2. The relevant sample sizes are 1,797, 866, and 504 after exclusion of all cases with any missing data for the largest model. The major source of loss in this listwise deletion of cases is the preliminary coding of industry to which we had access.

3. Originally we included earlier work experience (18–23), but it appeared to be insignificant (and had more missing values) and therefore it was dropped.

4. Shop workers are not in the reference group, but they are grouped with less skilled service workers rather than clerical workers as in the Registrar General's Social Class scheme, to reflect their relatively humble labor-market status, at least among women (Joshi and Newell 1987; Harrop and Joshi 1994).

5. Note also that the definition of an occupation as "feminized" is arbitrarily set at over 50% women in the national data. It is possible that taking a different cut-off (say 70% or 80%) or a continuous indicator of sex composition could produce different results.

6. F values were 5.23, 1.88, and 2.41 for tests of structural difference in the parameters of the earnings equations of (1) the three groups, (2) the full-timers, and (3) the part-timers respectively. Since the degrees of freedom were [9,3198], [9,2701] and [9,1369]—leading to a critical value of F of 1.88 at 5% significant level—the hypothesis of the coefficients being the same across groups can be rejected.

7. The test of structural stability did not allow us to reject the hypothesis that they may share common parameters on these firm characteristics; the F-value was 0.80, against a critical value of 1.75 for [13,1335] degrees of freedom.

8. At the geometric mean.

Chapter 6

1. Blank (1990), however, concluded that selection into part-time work plays an important role in explaining pay differentials between full-timers and part-timers.

2. Macran (1993) reviews social and psychological literature on the hypotheses of effects on health of role "overload" or "enhancement." She finds more support for "enhancement."

3. These weights are not the only ones possible. As with any index number, results could differ with other weights.

4. The weights are given by the distribution of the childless and mothers within full-timers.

5. The existence of structural differences in the parameters is then tested using traditional F-tests. Whenever the F-test does not allow us to reject the hypothesis H_0 that the coefficients are the same, the relevant samples are pooled in a single equation allowing only for differences in the constant and the selection terms.

6. Of course what we cannot test is whether it is the predominance of low-productivity, low-effort mothers in this employment status that pushes down the pay of all part-timers.

Neither do we explore what it is that leads the few childless part-timers into this low-paid employment status.

7. Tests of the structural stability of the slope coefficients in the four equations together give F-values as follows: 3.23 for MRC—with 27 and 540 degrees of freedom; and 2.64 for NCDS—with 27 and 1,705 degrees of freedom. The relevant critical value is around 1.5 for both cohorts.

8. The absolute number is only 31 in the MRC sample, though they are relatively more abundant here than in the NCDS (43), which has a larger sample size overall.

9. These figures appear in the top right of the second panel for each survey, under the heading "parameter gap."

10. This time the order of the test was reversed compared to note 7. The F-values within part-timers and full-timers in NCDS are 1.56 and 1.67 respectively, and for MRC the value for part-timers and full-timers is 2.65 and 1.56, with critical values of 1.88 for both samples.

11. They also appear to share the selection term, λ, since the coefficient of its interaction term with the childless dummy is not statistically different from zero. The λ term itself is significant only for the part-timers in NCDS at the 5% level and at 1% for the small sample of MRC childless women working part-time. This suggests that selection into different employment/parental status has limited biasing effects on measured wages.

12. This does not mean that such policies were necessarily ineffective, as the position of mothers might have deteriorated in the absence of such policies. See Waldfogel (1997b), who finds that in the United States young mothers earned 83% of the pay of childless women in 1980, as compared to 80% in 1991; in log points the difference increased from 0.183 to 0.214.

13. Given the very small number of part-timers without children in both cohorts, one should not draw firm conclusions about the "within part-timers" differential.

14. Occupational history data for women in NCDS were not coded in time for this topic to be investigated in the present study, but evidence from the PSI Maternity Rights Studies (McRae 1995) suggests that returning to a part-time job after a break was still, in the early 1990s, associated with downward occupational mobility. Continuous employment trajectories, facilitated by maternity leave, were not.

15. The way the employment histories were reported makes it impossible to tell whether women actually took maternity leave. This should have been reported as a continuous spell of employment, but was not always. Mothers who reported no interruption almost certainly had some leave. Those who reported breaks under twelve months may well have done so. Unlike Waldfogel (1995), we did not attempt to distinguish those who would have been eligible.

16. In addition to using revised data, this paper differs from her study of the NCDS data set in various details. The maternity leave variable in Waldfogel's (1995) study refers to periods of interruption around the time of the most recent birth, while in this paper it refers to the first. We allow and test for structural differences in all parameters of the earnings equations of mothers, with and without maternity leave, and childless women. We separate women working full-time from those employed part-time since our tests suggest strongly significant structural differences in the way human capital characteristics are remunerated in the two markets.

17. The relevant F-test was 0.26 for 18,3890 degrees of freedom.

References

Aigner, D. J., and G. C. Cain. 1977. Statistical theories of discrimination. *Industrial and Labour Relations Review* 30(2): 175–187.

Bartley, M., D. Blane, and J. Charlton. 1997. Socio-economic and demographic trends, 1841–1991. In J. Charlton and M. Murphy, eds., *The Health of Adult Britain*. London: HMSO, pp 74–92.

Becker, G. 1957 (2d ed., 1971). *The Economics of Discrimination*. Chicago: University of Chicago Press.

Becker, G. S. 1981 (revised and enlarged, 1991). *A Treatise on the Family*. Cambridge, MA: Harvard University Press.

Becker, G. 1985. Human capital, effort, and the sexual division of labour. *Journal of Labor Economics* 3: 553–558.

Bellace, J. R. 1991. The role of the law in effecting gender pay equality: a comparison of six countries' experience. In S. L. Willborn, ed., *Women's Wages: Stability and Change in Six Industrial Countries*. Greenwich, CN: JAI Press, pp. 21–37.

Bergmann, B. R. 1971. Occupational segregation, wages, and profits when employers discriminate by race or sex. *Eastern Economic Journal* 1: 103–110.

Blackburn, M. et al. 1990. What can explain the increase in earnings inequality among males? *Industrial Relations* 29(3): 441–456.

Blackaby, D. H., K. Clark, D. G. Lester, and P. D. Murphy, 1994. Black-white male earnings, employment prospects, and the earnings distribution: Evidence for Britain. *Economics Letters* 46: 273–279.

Blackaby, D. H., K. Clark, D. G. Lester, and P. D. Murphy, 1997. The distribution of male and female earnings, 1973–91: Evidence for Britain. *Oxford Economic Papers* 49: 256–272.

Blank, R. 1990. Are part-time jobs bad jobs? In G. Burtless, ed., *A Future of Lousy Jobs?* Washington, D.C.: Brookings Institution.

Blau, F. D., and M. Ferber. 1987. Discrimination: Empirical evidence from the United States. *American Economic Review, Papers and Proceedings* 77(2): 316–320.

Blau, F. D., and L. M. Kahn. 1994. The gender earnings gap: Some international evidence. In R. B. Freeman and L. Katz, eds., *Differences and Changes in Wage Structures*. Chicago: University of Chicago Press.

Blinder, A. S. 1973. Wage discrimination: Reduced form and structural variables. *Journal of Human Resources* 8: 436–465.

Bloom, D. E., and M. R. Killingsworth. 1982. Pay discrimination research and litigation: The use of regression. *Industrial Relations* 21(3): 318–339.

Borooah, V., and L. Lee. 1988. The effect of changes in Britain's industrial structure on female relative pay and employment. *Economic Journal* 98: 818–832.

Booth, A. L. 1995. *The Economics of the Trade Union*. Cambridge: Cambridge University Press.

Bosworth, D., P. Dawkins, and T. Stromback. 1996. *The Economics of the Labour Market*. Harlow: Longman.

Bradshaw, J., S. Kennedy, M. Kilkey, S. Hutton, A. Corden, T. Eardley, H. Holmes, and J. Neale. 1996. *The Employment of Lone Parents: A Comparison of Policy in Twenty Countries*. London: Family Policy Studies Centre.

Brown, R. S., M. Moon, and B. Zoloth. 1980. Incorporating occupational attainments in studies of male-female differential. *Journal of Human Resources* 15(1): 3–28.

Brown, W. 1993. The contraction of collective bargaining in Britain. *British Journal of Industrial Relations* 31: 189–200.

Bruegel, I., and D. Perrons. 1995. Where do the costs of unequal treatment for women fall? An analysis of the incidence of the costs of unequal pay and sex discrimination in the UK. In J. Humphreys and J. Rubery, eds., *The Economics of Equal Opportunities*. Manchester: Equal Opportunities Commission, pp. 155–174.

Butler, N., and D. Bonham. 1963. *Perinatal Mortality*. Edinburgh: Livingstone.

Butler, N., and J. Golding, 1986. *From Birth to Five*. Oxford: Pergamon.

Bynner, J., and E. Ferri, eds. 1997. *Twenty-something in the 1990s: Getting on, Getting by, Getting Nowhere*. Aldershot: Dartmouth.

Bynner, J., L. Morphy, and S. Parsons. 1996. *Women, Employment, and Skills*. NCDS Working Paper 44, SSRU, City University.

Charlton, J., and M. Murphy, eds. 1997. *The Health of Adult Britain*. London: HMSO.

Cherry, N. 1984a. Women and work stress: evidence from the 1946 birth cohort. *Ergonomics* 27: 519–526.

Cherry, N. 1984b. Nervous strain, anxiety, and symptoms amongst 32-year-old men at work in Britain. *Journal of Occupational Psychology* 57: 95–105.

Chiswick, B. R. 1973. Racial discrimination and the labour market: a test of alternative hypotheses. *Journal of Political Economy* 81: 1330–1352.

Cigno, A. 1991. *The Economics of the Family*. Oxford: Clarendon Press.

Corcoran, M., G. Duncan, and M. Ponza. 1983. A longitudinal analysis of white women's wages. *Journal of Human Resources* 18, 1 (Winter): 497–520.

Dale, A., and M. Egerton. 1997. *Highly Educated Women: Evidence from the National Child Development Study*. Research Report No. RS25. Sheffield: Department for Education and Employment.

Davies, H. 1997. Testing for sample selection bias amongst women working full-time. In A. Dale and M. Egerton *Highly Educated Women: Evidence from the National Child Development Study*. Research Report No. RS25. Sheffield: Department for Education and Employment, pp. 125–133.

Davies, H. B., and H. E. Joshi. 1998. Gender and income inequality in the UK: 1968–1990: feminization of earning or of poverty? *Journal of the Royal Statistical Society, Series A*. 161: 33–61.

De Cooman, E., J. F. Ermisch, and H. E. Joshi. 1987. The next birth and the labour market: A dynamic econometric model of births in England and Wales. *Population Studies* 41(2): 237–268.

Dex, S. 1987. *Women's Occupational Mobility*. London: Macmillan.

Dex, S., and R. Sewell. 1995. Equal opportunities policies and women's labour market status in industrialised countries. In J. Humphreys and J. Rubery, eds. *The Economics of Equal Opportunities*. Manchester: Equal Opportunities Commission, pp. 367–392.

Dex, S., H. Joshi, and S. Macran. 1996. A widening gulf among Britain's mothers. *Oxford Review of Economic Policy* 12: 65–75.

Disney, R., A. Gosling, and S. Machin. 1995. British unions in decline: Determinants of the 1980s' fall in recognition. *Labour and Labour Relations Review* 48: 48–91.

Dolton, P. J., and G. H. Makepeace. 1985. The statistical measurement of discrimination. *Economic Letters* 18: 391–395.

Dolton, P., and G. Makepeace. 1986. Sample selection and male-female earnings differentials in the graduate labour market. *Oxford Economic Papers* 38: 317–341.

Dolton, P., and G. Makepeace. 1987. Marital status, child rearing, and earnings differentials in the graduate labour market. *Economic Journal* 97: 897–922.

Douglas, J. W. B. 1964. *The Home and the School*. London: MacGibbon and Kee.

Douglas, J. W. B. 1976. The use and abuse of national cohorts. In M. Shipman, ed., *The Organisation and Impact of Social Research*. London: Routledge.

Edgeworth, F. Y. 1922. Equal pay to men and women for equal work. *Economic Journal* 32: 431–457.

European Commission. 1994. Employment Observatory. *Tableau de Bord (Synoptic Table)*. Directorate General of Employment, Industrial Relations, and Social Affairs, No. 2.

Ekinsmyth, C. 1996. The British longitudinal birth cohort studies: Their utility for the study of health and place. *Health and Place* 2(1): 15–26.

Ekinsmyth, C., J. Bynner, S. Montgomery, and P. Shepherd. 1992. *An Integrated Approach to the Design and Analysis of the 1970 British Cohort Study (BCS70) and the National Child Development Study (NCDS)*. SSRU Inter-Cohort Analysis Working Paper Series, Paper No. 1. London: City University.

Elias, P., and M. Gregory. 1994. *The Changing Structure of Occupations and Earnings in Great Britain, 1975–1990: An Analysis Based on the New Earnings Survey Panel Dataset*. Research Series No. 27. London: Employment Department.

Equal Opportunities Commission. 1994. *Black and Ethnic Minority Women and Men in Britain, 1994*. Manchester: Equal Opportunities Commission.

Equal Opportunities Commission. 1995. *Annual Report of the Equal Opportunities Commission for 1994*. Manchester: Equal Opportunities Commission.

Equal Opportunities Commission. 1996. *Building Equality into Everyday life: Annual Report of the Equal Opportunities Commission for 1995*. Manchester: Equal Opportunities Commission.

Ermisch, J. F., H. E. Joshi, and R. E. Wright. 1991. Women's wages in Great Britain. In S. L. Willborn, ed., *Women's Wages: Stability and Change in Six Industrial Countries*. Greenwich, CN: JAI Press, pp. 221–240.

Ermisch, J. F., and R. E. Wright. 1992. Differential returns to human capital in full-time and part-time employment. In N. Folbre et al., eds., *Women's Work in the World Economy*. London: Macmillan, pp. 195–212.

Ermisch, J. F., and R. E. Wright. 1993. Wage offers and full-time and part-time employment by British women. *Journal of Human Resources* 28: 111–133.

Esping-Anderson, G. 1990. *Three Worlds of Welfare Capitalism*. Princeton, NJ: Princeton University Press.

Fallick, J. L., and R. F. Elliot, eds. 1981. *Incomes Policy, Inflation, and Relative Pay*. London: George Allen and Unwin.

Felstead, A. 1995. The gender implications of creating a training market: Alleviating or reinforcing inequality of access? In J. Humphreys and J. Rubery, eds. *The Economics of Equal Opportunities*. Manchester: Equal Opportunities Commission, pp. 177–201.

Ferri, E., ed. 1993. *Life at 33: The Fifth Follow-up of the National Child Development Study*. London: National Children's Bureau.

Fogelman, K. 1983. *Growing Up in Great Britain: Collected Papers from the National Child Development Study*. London: Macmillan.

Fogelman, K., and P. Wedge. 1981. The National Child Development Study (1958 British cohort). In: S. Mednick and A. Baert, eds. *Prospective Longitudinal Research in Europe: An Empirical Basis for Primary Prevention*. Oxford: Oxford University Press.

Folbre, N. 1994. *Who Pays for the Kids? Gender and the Structures of Constraint*. London: Routledge.

Freeman, C. 1982. The understanding employer. In J. West, ed., *Work, Women, and the Labor Market*. London: Routledge and Kegan Paul.

Fuchs, V. 1988. *Women's Quest for Economic Equality*. Cambridge, MA: Harvard University Press.

Gill, A. M. 1994. Incorporating the causes of occupational differences in studies of race wage differentials. *Journal of Human Resources* 241(1): 20–41.

Gill, T. 1995. New rights for part-time workers: Making the case for fair treatment at work. London: TUC.

Goodman, A., and S. Webb. 1994. For richer, for poorer: The changing distribution of income in the UK, 1961–91. *Fiscal Studies* 15: 29–62.

Gosling, A., S. Machin, and C. Meghir. 1994. What has happened to men's wages since the mid-60s? *Fiscal Studies* 15, (4): 111–133.

Green, F., S. Machin, and A. Manning. 1996. The employer-size wage effect: Can dynamic monopsony provide an explanation? *Oxford Economic Papers* 48(3): 433—455.

Greene, W. 1992. *Limdep Version 6.0, User Manual and Reference Guide*. Econometric Software, Inc.

Greenhalgh, C. 1980. Male-female wage differentials: Is marriage an equal opportunity? *Economic Journal* 90: 751—775.

Gregg, P., and S. Machin. 1995. Is the rise in UK inequality different? In R. Barrel, ed., *The UK Labour Market*. Cambridge: Cambridge University Press.

Gronau, R. 1988. Sex-related wage differentials and women's interrupted labor careers—the chicken or the egg? *Journal of Labor Economics* 6(3): 277—301.

Groshen, E. L. 1991. The structure of the female/male wage differential. *Journal of Human Resources* 26(3): 457—472.

Gunderson, M. 1989. Male-female wage differentials and policy responses. *Journal of Economic Literature* 27(1): 46—72.

Gunderson, M., and R. E. Robb. 1991. Legal and institutional issues pertaining to women's wages in Canada. In S. L. Willborn, ed., *International Review of Comparative Public Policy*, 3, pp. 129—150. Greenwich, CT: JAI Press Inc.

Hakim, C. 1991. Grateful slaves and self-made women: Fact and fantasy in women's work orientations. *European Sociological Review* 8: 127—152.

Hakim, C. 1996. *Key Issues in Women's Work: Female Heterogeneity and the Polarisation of Women's Employment*. London and Atlantic Heights, NJ: Athlone.

Hanlon, J. 1996. Indirect discrimination and equal pay: The European dimension. Typescript, Nene College, Northampton.

Harkness, S. 1996. The gender earnings gap: Evidence from the UK. *Fiscal Studies* 17: 1—36.

Harkness, S., and S. Machin. 1995. Changes in women's wages in Britain: What has happened to the male-female differential since the mid-1970s? Mimeo, Centre for Economic Performance, London School of Economics.

Harkness, S., S. Machin, and J. Waldfogel. 1997. Evaluating the pin money hypothesis. *Journal of Population Economics* 10: 137—158.

Harper, B., and M. Haq. 1995. Occupational attainment in Britain: The role of ability and status. Mimeo, London Guildhall University.

Harrop, A., and H. Joshi. 1994. Death and the saleswoman: An invesigation of mortality and occupational immobility of women in the Longitudinal Study of England and Wales. LS Working Paper 73, SSRU, City University.

Heckman, J. 1979. Sample selection bias as specification error. *Econometrica* 47: 151—161.

Heitlinger, A. 1993. *Women's Equality, Demography, and Public Policy: A Comparative Perspective*. New York: St. Martin's Press.

Hildreth, A. K. G. 1997. Instrument and measurement error in the estimation of union wage effect for covered members and non-members in Great Britain. Working Paper 97-5, ESRC Research Centre on Micro-Social Change, University of Essex.

Hill, M. 1979. The wage effects of marital status and children. *Journal of Human Resources* 14(4): 579–594.

Hills, J. C. 1995. *Inquiry into Income and Wealth, Vol. 2.* Joseph Rowntree Foundation, York.

Humphries, J., and J. Rubery. 1995. Some lessons for policy. In J. Humphries and J. Rubery, eds., pp. 393–405.

Humphries, J., and J. Rubery, eds., 1995. *The Economics of Equal Opportunities.* Manchester: Equal Opportunities Commission.

Hunter, L., and S. Rimmer. 1995. An exploration of the UK and Australian experiences. In J. Humphries and J. Rubery, eds., pp. 245–274.

Jenkins, S. P. 1994. Earnings discrimination measurement. *Journal of Econometrics* 61: 81–102.

Johnson, P., and H. Reed. 1996. Intergenerational mobility among the rich and the poor: Results from the National Child Development Study. *Oxford Review of Economic Policy* 12(1): 127–142.

Joint Committee of the Royal College of Obstetricians and Gynaecologists and the Population Investigation Committee [Joint Committee (a)]. 1948. *Maternity in Great Britain.* London: Oxford University Press.

Jones, E., and J. Long. 1979. Part-week work and human capital investment by married women. *Journal of Human Resources* 14, 4 (Fall): 563–578.

Joshi, H. E. 1991. Sex and motherhood as sources of women's economic disadvantage. In D. Groves and M. Maclean, eds., *Women's Issues in Social Policy.* London: Routledge, pp. 179–193.

Joshi, H. 1996. Combining employment and childrearing, the story of British women's lives. In A. Offer, ed., *Perspectives on the Quality of Life.* Oxford: Oxford University Press, pp. 88–118.

Joshi, H. 1998. The opportunity costs of childbearing: More than mothers' business? *Journal of Population Economics* 11: (in press).

Joshi, H., A. Dale, C. Ward, and H. Davies. 1995. *Dependence and Independence in the Finances of Women at Age 33.* London: Family Policy Studies Centre.

Joshi H., and H. Davies 1996. Financial dependency on men. Have women born in 1958 broken free? *Policy Studies* 17, 1: 35–54.

Joshi, H., H. Davies, and H. Land. 1996. *The Tale of Mrs. Typical,* Occasional Paper 21. London: Family Policy Studies Centre.

Joshi, H., S. Dex, and S. Macran. 1996. Employment over childbearing and women's subsequent labour force participation: Evidence from the 1958 birth cohort. *Journal of Population Economics* 9: 325–348.

Joshi, H. E., and P. R. A. Hinde. 1993. Employment after childbearing: Cohort study evidence. *European Sociological Review* 9: 203–227.

Joshi, H. E., P. R. G. Layard, and S. J. Owen. 1985. Why are more women working in Britain? *Journal of Labor Economics* 3 (January): S147–S176.

Joshi, H. E., and M-L. Newell. 1987. Job downgrading after childbearing. In M. Uncles, ed., *London Papers in Regional Science 18. Longitudinal Data Analysis: Methods and Applications.* London: Pion, pp. 89–102.

Joshi, H., and M-L. Newell. 1989. *Pay Differentials and Parenthood: Analysis of Men and Women Born in 1946*. Institute of Employment Research Report. Coventry: University of Warwick.

Joshi, H., and S. J. Owen. 1987. How long is a piece of elastic? The measurement of female activity rates in British censuses. *Cambridge Journal of Economics* 11, 1: 55–74.

Joshi, H., and P. Paci. 1997. Life in the labour market. In J. Bynner and E. Ferri, eds., *Twenty-something in the 1990s: Getting On, Getting By, Getting Nowhere*. Aldershot: Dartmouth, 31–52.

Juster, T., and F. Stafford. 1991. The allocation of time: Empirical findings, behavioural models, and problems of measurement. *Journal of Economic Literature* 29: 491–522.

Kiernan, K. E. 1986. Teenage marriage and marital breakdown: A longitudinal study. *Population Studies* 40: 35–54.

Kiernan, K. E. 1992. The impact of family disruption in childhood on transitions made in young adult life. *Population Studies* 46, 2: 213–234.

Kiernan, K. E. 1997. Becoming a young parent: A longitudinal study of associated factors. *British Journal of Sociology* 46: 406–428.

Kiernan, K. E., and I. D. Diamond. 1983. The age at which childbearing starts: A longitudinal study. *Population Studies* 37: 363–380.

Killingsworth, M. R. 1987. Heterogeneous preferences, compensating wage differentials, and comparable worth. *Quarterly Journal of Economics* 102(4): 727–742.

Killingsworth, M. R. 1990. *The Economics of Comparable Worth*. Kalamazoo, MI: Upjohn Institute.

Killingsworth, M. R. 1993. Analyzing employment discrimination: From the seminar room to the courtroom. *American Economic Review* 83(2): 67–72.

Korenman, S., and D. Neumark. 1992. Marriage, motherhood, and wages. *Journal of Human Resources* 26: 233–255.

Kuh, D., and Y. Ben Shlomo, eds. 1997. *A Lifecourse Approach to Chronic Disease Epidemiology: Tracing the Origins of Ill Health from Early to Adult Life*. Oxford: Oxford University Press.

Kuh, D. L., J. Head, R. Hardy, and M. E. J. Wadsworth. 1997. The influences of education and family background on women's earnings in mid-life: Evidence from a British Birth Cohort Study. *British Journal of Sociology of Education* 18(3): 385–405.

Lewis, G. H. 1986. Union relative wage-effect. In O. Ashefelter and P. R. G. Layard, eds., *Handbook of Labour Economics*, vol. 2. Amsterdam: North Holland.

Lissenburgh, S. 1996. *Value for Money: The Costs and Benefits of Giving Part-time Workers Equal Rights*. Report from PSI to the TUC.

Löfström, Å. 1996. Variation in female activity and employment patterns: The case of Sweden. Umeå Economic Studies no 407, Umeå University.

Machin, S., and A. Manning. 1994. The effect of minimum-wages on wage dispersion and employment: Evidence from the U.K. wages councils. *Industrial and Labour Relations Review* 47(2): 319–329.

Maclean, M., and M. Wadsworth. 1988. The interests of children after parental divorce: A long-term perspective. *International Journal of Law and the Family* 2: 155–166.

Macran, S. 1993. Role Enhancement or Role Overload? A Review of Research on the Health Consequences of Women's Domestic and Paid Work. CPS Research Paper 93-1, London School of Hygiene and Tropical Medicine.

Macran, S., H. Joshi, and S. Dex. 1996. Employment after childbearing: A survival analysis. *Work, Employment, and Society* 10(2): 273–296.

Manning, A. 1996. The Equal Pay Act as an experiment to test theories of the labour market. *Economica* 663: 191–212.

Makepeace, G. H., P. Paci, H. Joshi, and P. J. Dolton. 1997. How unequally has equal pay progressed in the 1980s: A study of two British cohorts. typescript, City University.

Martin, J., and C. Roberts. 1984. *Women and Employment: A Lifetime Perspective*. London: H.M.S.O.

McRae, S. 1995. *Women's Employment during Family Formation*. Policy Studies Institute Report. London: Policy Studies Institute.

McCrudden, C. 1991. Between legality and reality: The implementation of equal pay for work of equal value in Great Britain. In Willborn, S. L., ed., *Women's Wages: Stability and Change in Six Industrial Countries*. Greenwich, CT: JAI Press.

Miller, P. W. 1987. The wage effect of the occupational segregation of women. *Economic Journal* 97: 885–896.

Millward, N., and S. Woodland. 1995. Gender segregation and male/female wage differentials. In J. Humphries and J. Rubery, eds., pp. 221–244.

Mincer, J. 1985. Intercountry comparisons of labour force trends and of related devlopments: An overview. *Journal of Labor Economics* 3: S1–S32.

Mincer, J., and S. Polachek. 1974. Family investments in human capital: earnings of women. *Journal of Political Economy* 82(2): S76–S108.

NCDS User Support Group. 1995. *Publications Arising from the National Child Development Study*. Working Paper 2, NCDS User Support Group, SSRU, and Librarian, National Children's Bureau.

Ní Bhrolcháin, M. 1986. Women's paid work and the timing of births. *European Journal of Population* 2: 43–70.

Neumark, D., and S. Korenman. 1994. Sources of bias in women's wage equations: Results using sibling data. *Journal of Human Resources* 29: 379–405.

Oaxaca, R. 1973. Male-female wage differentials in urban labour markets. *International Economic Review* 14(3): 693–709.

OECD. 1985. *The Integration of Women in the Economy*. Paris: OECD.

OECD. 1988. *Employment Outlook 1988*. Paris: OECD.

Office of National Statistics (ONS). 1997. *Labor Force Survey Historical Supplement*.

Olsen, R. J. 1994. Fertility and the size of the U.S. labor force. *Journal of Economic Literature* 32 (March): 60–100.

Ostner, I. 1993. Slow motion: Women, work, and the family in Germany. In J. Lewis, ed., *Women and Social Policies in Europe: Work, Family, and the State*, pp. 92–115. Aldershot: Edward Elgar.

Paci, P. 1997. NCDS Job Histories: Employment Status 1974–1991. NCDS Data Note 4, SSRU, City University.

Paci, P., H. Joshi, and G. Makepeace. 1995. Pay gaps facing men and women born in 1958: Differences within the labour market. In J. Humphries and J. Rubery, eds., *The Economics of Equal Opportunity*. Manchester: Equal Opportunities Commission, pp. 87–111.

Paci, P., and H. Joshi. 1996. *Wage Differentials between Men and Women: Evidence from the Birth Cohort Studies*. Research Report 71, Sheffield: Department for Education and Employment.

Phelps, E. S. 1972. The statistical theory of racism and sexism. *American Economic Review* 62: 659–661.

Power, C., O. Manor, and J. Fox. 1991. *Health and Class: The Early Years*. London: Chapman Hall.

Reagan, R. B. 1978. Two supply curves for economists. Implication of mobility and career attachment of women. *American Economic Review* 65: 100–107.

Rosen, S. 1986. The theory of equalizing differences. In O. Ashfelter and P. R. G. Layard, eds. *Handbook of Labour Economics*, vol. 1, Amsterdam: North Holland, pp. 641–692.

Rosholm, M., and N. Smith. 1996. The Danish gender wage gap in the 1980s: A panel study. *Oxford Economic Papers* 48: 254–279.

Schmitt, J. 1995. The changing structure of male earnings in Britain, 1974–88. London School of Economics, forthcoming in R. Freeman and L. Katz, eds., *Changes and Differences in Wage Structures*. Chicago: University of Chicago Press.

Shepherd, P. 1993. Analysis of response bias. In Ferri, ed., *Life at 33: The Fifth Follow-up of the National Child Development Study*. London: National Children's Bureau, pp. 184–187.

Siebert, J., and W. S. Addison. 1991. Internal labour markets: Causes and comparisons. *Oxford Review of Economic Policy* 7(1): 76–92.

Sloane, P. J. 1990. Sex differentials: Structure stability, and change. In M. B. Gregory, and A. W. J. Thomson, eds., *A Portrait of Pay, 1970–1982: An Analysis of the New Earnings Survey*, pp. 125–171.

Sloane, P. and I. Theodossiou. 1994. A generalised Lorenz curve approach to explaining the upward movement in women's relative earnings in Britain. *Scottish Journal of Political Economy* 41: 464–476.

Stewart, M., and C. Greenhalgh. 1984. Work history patterns and the occupational attainment of women. *Economic Journal* 94(375): 493–519.

Stiglitz, J. 1973. Approaches to the economics of discrimination. *American Economic Review, Papers, and Proceedings* 63: 287–295.

Thompson, N. P., S. M. Montgomery, R. E. Pounder, and A. J. Wakefield. 1995. Is measles vaccination a risk factor for inflammatory bowel disease? *The Lancet* 345: 1071–1074.

Timæus, I., and H. Joshi. 1983. Female survey members' employment and fertility histories from the National Survey of Health and Development. CPS/NS/19. Typescript, Centre for Population Studies, London School of Hygiene and Tropical Medicine.

Wadsworth, M. E. J. 1991. *The Imprint of Time: Childhood, History, and Adult life.* Oxford: Clarendon Press.

Wadsworth, M. E. J., M. Maclean, D. Kuh, and B. Rodgers. 1991. Children of divorced and separated parents: A summary and review of findings from a long-term follow-up study in the UK. *Sauvegarde de L'Enfance* 46: 152–161.

Wadsworth, M. E. J., C. Peckham, and B. Taylor. 1984. The role of national longitudinal studies in the prediction of health, development, and behaviour. In D. Walker and J. Richmond, eds., *Monitoring Child Health in the United States.* Cambridge, MA: Harvard University Press.

Wadsworth, M. E. J., and D. Kuh. 1997. Childhood influences on adult health: A review of recent work from the British 1946 Birth Cohort Study, the MRC National Survey of Health and Development. *Paediatry and Perinatal Epidemiology* 11: 2–20.

Waldfogel, J. 1993. Women working for less: A longitudinal analysis of the family gap. Welfare State Working Paper 93, STICERD, London School of Economics.

Waldfogel, J. 1995. The price of motherhood: Family status and women's pay in a young British cohort. *Oxford Economic Papers* 47: 584–610.

Waldfogel, J. 1997a. The wage effects of children. *American Sociological Review* 62: 209–217.

Waldfogel, J. 1997b. Working mothers then and now: A cross-cohort analysis of the effects of maternity leave on women's pay. In F. Blau and R. Ehrenberg, eds., *Gender and Family Issues in the Workplace.* New York: Russell Sage.

Waldfogel, J. 1998. The family gap for young women in the United States and Britain: Can maternity leave make a difference? *Journal of Labor Economics,* forthcoming.

Ward, C., A. Dale, and H. Joshi. 1993. Participation in the labour market. In E. Ferri, ed., *Life at 33: The Fifth Follow-up of the National Child Development Study.* London: National Children's Bureau, pp. 60–91.

Ward, C., A. Dale, and H. Joshi. 1996. Combining employment with child care: An escape from dependence? *Journal of Social Policy* 25(2): 223–247.

Willborn, S. 1989. *A Secretary and a Cook: Challenging Women's Wages in the Courts of the United States and Great Britain.* Ithaca, NY: ILR Press, Cornell University.

Willborn, S. L., ed. 1991. *Women's Wages: Stability and Change in Six Industrial Countries.* Greenwich, CT: JAI Press.

Willborn, S. L. 1991. Economic and legal perspectives on women's wages in six countries: An overview. In S. L. Willborn, ed., pp. 1–17.

Wood, R. G., M. E. Corcoran, and P. N. Courant. 1993. Pay differences among the highly paid: The male-female earnings gap in lawyers' salary. *Journal of Labor Economics* 11(3): 417–441.

Wright, R. E., and J. F. Ermisch. 1991. Gender discrimination in the British labour market: A reassessment. *Economic Journal* 101(406): 508–552.

Zabalza, A., and J. L. Arrufat. 1985. The extent of sex discrimination in Great Britain. In A. Zabalza, and Z. Tzannatos, eds., *Women and Equal Pay: The Effects of Legislation on Female Employment and Wages in Britain*, pp. 70–96.

Zabalza, A., and Z. Tzannatos. 1986. *Women and Equal Pay: The Effect of Legislation on Female Employment and Wages in Britain*. Cambridge: Cambridge University Press.

Zellner, H. 1972. Discrimination against women, occupational segregation, and the relative wage. *American Economic Review* 62: 157–60.

Index

DEMCO